ADVENTURES
IN
INNOVATION

INSIDE THE RISE AND FALL OF NORTEL

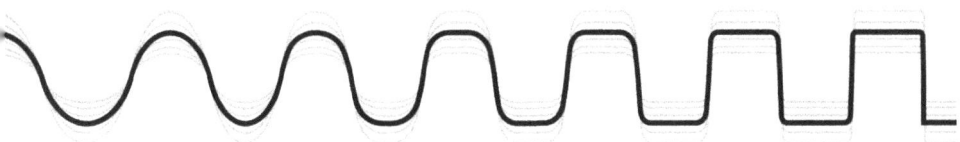

JOHN F. TYSON

Adventures in Innovation: Inside the Rise and Fall of Nortel

1st Edition

ISBN: 978-0-9936193-0-4
ISBN: 978-0-9936193-1-1 (eBook)

Adventures in Innovation

Email: info@adventuresininnovation.ca
Website: www.adventuresininnovation.ca

This book is recyclable.
Printed in the United States of America

DEDICATION

For the late Donald A. Chisholm, first president of Bell-Northern Research (BNR), a man of great intellect, wisdom, and vision who understood the gift of trust.

CONTENTS

ACKNOWLEDGMENTS

Writing this book was an adventure in its own right. Following my retirement from Nortel Networks, rehashing my career was the furthest thing from my mind. But once the decision was made and with no idea of where the adventure would lead, I discovered the need for an awful lot of help along the way. This book, to a great degree, is the result of a friends-and-family collaboration. Bless 'em, one and all. While listening to my rants and raves, they patiently coached me through the whole process from defining the initial structure to shaping the final manuscript.

To begin, I must thank my volunteer editors: Arnold Campbell, Eva-Jane Lark, and Edo Brandt. Their valuable insights and encouraging comments gave me fresh resolve during an often-arduous process. They lifted my spirit with comments such as: "Great stories. I laughed out loud" and "I love it...keep going."

My special thanks to friends and colleagues Phil Tillman, David Cuddy, Richard St. John, Velma LeBlanc, and Jacques Gagnon who dug deep into their own archives in order to expand my limited recollections. The result was a treasure trove of research material and fond memories.

I thank the entire Tyson family—Yolanda, Sean, Kevin, and Kyla—for their patience and accommodation during my emotional roller coaster rides from top to bottom and back again. Thank goodness for our long-standing family candor and sense of humour.

I am especially indebted to the team of Kyla Tyson and Adam Januszkiewicz who jumped in with all four feet and carried the copy editing, internal layout design, and publishing details all the way to book launch. Thanks also to Sean Tyson for all his work on the website and promotion.

Special praise is due to my editor, Greg Cable, whose substantive skills and insights impacted the book at every level. Unrelenting in his focus on chronology while representing the view of the general reader, he managed to bring a fragmented story together while maintaining my voice and tone.

I thank them all so very much.

INTRODUCTION

Innovation is defined in many ways. To simply say it's coming up with something new and different is accurate and easy. But to some, it's also the key to prosperity and the source of new wealth. Nations are waking up to innovation as a national priority essential for growth. It's the driver of productivity and the linchpin of success. Innovation is transformative, a process creating new careers and enriching communities at every level and in every way.

All true, and I know this because I spent 35 years inside a corporation where the research-and-development culture thrived in the spirit of innovation, dedication, and excellence. The R&D environment was my playground and I loved the collaboration that it nurtured and demanded. As a participant and witness to innovation, I learned many lessons still applicable today and had a lot of fun along the way. So to me, innovation will always be defined as a journey of discovery, delight, and fulfillment.

I thought a great deal about this, one cold day in January 2012. I had been invited to contribute to an extensive academic case study of how and why my playground—Nortel Networks and Bell-Northern Research (BNR), the wonderful world where I had spent my working life and where I had found and lived out my dreams—had simply passed away.

Two university faculty members joined me in the comfort of my living room for a delightful afternoon of wine and cheese in front of the fire. Armed with detailed sets of questions, they allowed me to rant and rave and laugh while keeping me focused on their assignment. The scheduled two-hour meeting turned into four hours of fun (with an additional bottle of wine). Satisfied they got what they came for, I thanked them and said good-bye at the front door. It was only after hearing the door click shut that I stopped to ask myself, "Is that it? As an insider, did I have more to say?" Hell yes. *Adventures in Innovation* is the result.

I had the privilege of working with extraordinary people through an exceptional period of innovation in the field of communications. These were great days in the history of a fundamental industry, and I was privileged to play a part. We took on big challenges and changed the world, guiding a technology revolution that continues to evolve in unexpected and fascinating ways.

The digital world we helped fashion has transformed commerce by creating an alternate media channel for the distribution of goods and services. The web and smart phones have created social networking as a category of e-commerce, giving the end user a lot more control. The ease, speed, plus the breadth and depth of access has shattered the conventional business models of entertainment, news media, education, banking, retail, and every field of applied scientific research. Industries are being forced to innovate and adapt, or die. Even as the new market matures and consolidates, wealth is being created. Innovation breeds innovation, and the change we're experiencing is just a taste of what is yet to come.

I believe that there's a generation gap that challenges our understanding of high-tech business and innovation today. My observations come from watching my own children and their peers enter the working world, living testimony to the impact of the web and mobility. They are part of a younger generation (I can't help but think of them as "the kids") who were born in the 1980s and have come into their own in the new millennium.

Theirs is the first generation that grew up in a digital world. Surrounded by digital media from birth, they simply take for granted the discontinuity created by digital technology and use it as the base platform for applied research. They have a different outlook and a different attitude, and work and play in different ways. They are fundamentally changing the nature of commerce and marketing, inventing new business practices, and reshaping society. The discontinuity created by the Internet, web, and mobility has shattered traditional business models, lowering the barriers to entry and compressing the interval to market.

In their mid-20s to early 30s, the world is their oyster. Given the state of the current economy, they know that job security is a thing of the past, but they have faith in themselves and live in the moment. They are self-actualizing, expressing their creativity in new and innovative ways, pursuing new knowledge, exploring new spiritual dimensions, and contributing to their communities. Taking nothing for granted, they have their feet on the ground and their heads in the cloud (pun intended).

This digital generation lives in a world of software almost devoid of hardware. They outsource nothing, are clamoring for talent, and can gain speedy access to the talents of the best and brightest minds throughout the world. They accept that traditional models have been shattered by interactive digital media and are creating a new ecosystem for nurturing innovation. Moving faster than we can analyze, they simply innovate, earn, and learn by doing. With the innocence and vitality of youth, they retain a sense of wonder and delight, indeed adventure, working and playing hard, capitalizing on whatever opportunities they see, embracing risk, and having fun on the road to fulfillment.

Adaptive up-starts (a term I prefer to start-ups) are creating new businesses and careers, and are quietly functioning as angel investors incubating new start-ups. They are becoming local community leaders who hope to grow and thrive in collaborative communities close to home. Out of the gate, they think local while their talents and markets are global. They start small and think big.

Not content with convention, they have moved from suburban industrial parks to the most adaptable community for innovation, the urban core. They don't look for employee parking spaces, but provide bicycle racks. They have tossed workstations, buy office furniture from Ikea, and are often located in second story walk-ups above restaurants, bars, and small businesses. Numbering in the thousands, they can be found in the dynamic urban cores of San Francisco, Seattle, New York, Boston, Vancouver, Toronto, and Montreal. They're even waking up the formally somnolent Byward Market in my hometown of Ottawa.

Innovation is being reborn in a new incarnation. As the beneficiaries of the discontinuity and market disruption created by an earlier generation of innovators, these "kids" are unencumbered by history and are willing to imagine new possibilities. They are the embodiment of a new spirit and are setting off on new and exciting adventures.

I can only admire their attitudes and ambitions and wish them well. I love being around them because they remind me of how I felt in my youth as I entered and explored the dizzying new world of innovation.

Those adventures for me played out mainly in Ottawa where I spent much of my career. A community of extraordinary people gathered in the region in the latter part of the 20th century and founded an organization that, over the next 25 years, blossomed into a global powerhouse. Many of the younger generation don't realize that it was in Ottawa that much of the digital world was envisioned, designed, and built.

By recounting the adventures I experienced in my long quest for relevance and fulfillment, I can perhaps inspire others as they set off on similar quests. The spirit of innovation calls on us to believe in ourselves. While Ottawa's time as a global high-tech mecca has passed and its reputation has become slightly tarnished, I believe that the spirit that animated us still hovers above the city and the country, proudly engaged, nurturing a new generation of innovators with the creativity, imagination, and passion to define new opportunities and realize their visions.

1 FINDING A PLACE

I've often thought back on how my adventures began and when I first set out on my lifelong journey of discovery and delight. Well into retirement, I found a clue in a small steel box of items my mother had saved more than half-a-century before.

Inside was a clipping from the Ottawa Citizen newspaper from sometime in the late 1940s. It must have been a slow news day or simply an indication of what a sleepy government town Ottawa was in those days, as the clipping bore the headline: "Sand Castles Feature at McNabb Park." The article went on, "Castles, mountains and volcanoes, all formed by the small fry, decorated the sand box at McNabb Park yesterday as their second contest of the year took place. A dominating castle by John Tyson brought him first prize in the boys division for best design."

I was the six-year-old boy who took home the trophy. Looking at the clipping, I remembered the event and the pride I felt in telling my parents that I had won. I'm sure my imagination has made the "dominating castle" a masterpiece of design and much larger than it really was. Yet in my mind it stands as an icon, the very expression of my approach over the many decades to come: an innovative idea arising from the natural child within, an intuitive problem-solution-benefit analysis, and an inherent ability to execute. The realization that such elements would be critical to my career was a long time coming, however. It required years of exploration and learning critical life lessons along the way until I found my place in the community and the world.

I was a regular kid who managed to get through school by doing just more than enough to get by. We lived in Centretown and Cambridge Street Public School was only half a block from home. The small school was on the leading edge of education for its time, with special-needs classrooms for the hearing impaired and mentally challenged. We successfully shared the school, though the special classes tended to have older and bigger students. I discovered during more than one recess that I was attending the school of hard knocks.

The elementary years are something of a blur, though I recall often engaging my natural talents for music, art, and cartoons. I was always cartooning and my seasonal school drawings always made it onto the hallway walls. But my major love was music. I loved to sing, and the school choir was a natural match, leading to an audition for the boys' choir of nearby St. Luke's Anglican Church. St. Luke's followed the choral traditions of Westminster Abbey and Kings College, Cambridge, whose iconic boys' choirs filled the pews of Anglican cathedrals and whose liturgical traditions transferred to the Dominion of Canada. My angelic years were the most memorable of my childhood, encompassing my first career as a boy soprano. The life of a choirboy was not easy. It meant boys' practice on Wednesday, full choir practice Friday night, two services on Sunday, and, after being chosen to sing solo descant, an independent treble melody sung above the basic melody, frequent Saturday morning lessons with the choirmaster. My choral career taught me to appreciate the benefits of dedication and persistence.

I eventually became head choirboy. My first leadership role was keeping the rest of the boys ("the squirts") in line through the traditions passed down through the old-boy private boarding schools. Having suffered the crap (bullying) through three previous head boys, I was determined to be different. We were there to have fun and build on our common love of singing. Based on the time-honoured practice of cleaning the blackboard and brushes for the teacher, I rewarded good behavior by allowing the squirts to distribute the sheet music before practice and return it to the choirmaster's library. What a guy. My career as head choirboy ended when my voice cracked during a public performance of Handel's Messiah. Shortly after, I was, without ceremony, relegated to the back row with the tenors. A byproduct of my short career was acquiring the social graces required to deal with adults and other superiors beyond pinched cheeks and pats on the head.

On the whole, being occupied with church, school choirs, Boy Scouts, and a paper route, life during the elementary school years was secure and good.

Entering high school, as always, involved a culture shock. I suddenly found myself at the bottom of the ladder with the status of a "four-eyed" little creep (I wore glasses with thick lenses since Grade 1). Glebe Collegiate Institute streamed its students toward university and students could choose a liberal arts or science stream, each with compulsory courses such as English, history, and physical education, followed by courses of special interest. I chose the science stream combined with art and music.

Glebe C.I. was a great school with a longstanding culture and terrific spirit. On special days, and there were many, there could be anything from a sing-along to a pep rally for sports events, a band concert, or skits promoting upcoming dances. Football Fridays were always a big hit, with classes cancelled, a pep rally on the front lawn, and the whole school—including cheerleaders, marching band, and teachers—led by a police motorcycle escort marching the ten or twelve blocks to Lansdowne Park (home of the CFL's former Ottawa Roughriders) for the weekly intercollegiate match. The benefits of cultivating a joyful collaborative spirit among large groups of people were unmistakable.

I was not an outstanding scholar and my natural entry point into high school life was based on my talent in music and art. The head of the art department, Miss Norris, known to the students as "Blinkie" because of her poor eyesight, was a great art teacher and a mentor to the student-initiated drama club. She had a quiet demeanor and encouraged us to take risks and be creative. In her classes, I discovered the joy of graphics. I loved creating decorations for school dances and proms as well as posters, concert programs, and banners for every school event, often illustrated with my cartoons. Art was so easy for me that the class was my way of holding up my overall grade average. I was also selected to attend an art program for gifted students on Saturday mornings for a couple of years at the National Gallery of Canada. But music consumed most of my available time and energy. The head of the music department, Mr. Berry—Sam—was a flamboyant natural leader. He taught music theory and appreciation, was proficient in every wind instrument, and took the band and glee club (called the Lyres Club) to a high performance standard. I thought of joining the glee club but there was no way I was going to audition until my voice changed completely. I instead chose to learn trombone and endured the excruciating noise of screeching clarinets.

I experienced my first life challenge when my father died from meningitis at 43. Thirteen at the time, I was adrift from Grade 9 to Grade 11. I maintained all extracurricular activities, but my school absences increased and my marks declined. My mother, unable to cope with my father's death, increasingly spent time with friends, leaving me alone for weeks at a time. I coped by simply immersing myself in daily life and not inviting anyone home.

My attendance record was eventually reported to the vice-principal, a former World War II tank commander and tough guy by reputation. Rather than report me for truancy, he came to my house to check out the circumstances. Home alone, I refused to answer the door. At school the next day, he intercepted me at the entrance and invited me into his office. While I appreciated his concern, I stormed out when he suggested I should consider foster care. A week later I was once again invited to his office, joined by the head of the math department. They asked if I would consider support from the Kiwanis Club and accept an invitation to live with the family of some great high school friends. I was shocked, but accepted on the spot.

Within days I was living with the family of Canon Henry Cook, an Anglican priest who would later become Bishop of the Arctic, the largest Anglican diocese in the world. Canon and Mrs. Cook (Opal) had three children: David, a student at Carleton University, and Peter and Barbara, fellow classmates at Glebe Collegiate. As parents, they were complementary. He was direct, no-nonsense, and quick-witted, while she, equally no-nonsense, had more patience and quietly nurtured. I was immediately accepted as one of the family: same rules and the same treatment if and when I stepped out of line. Their home was where students loved to gather after school and on weekends. Parental tolerance was high and parties were frequent.

We didn't have a curfew on weekends. We were trusted and simply needed to say where we were going and what time we expected to be home. I returned one Saturday night much later than expected and quietly climbed the stairs to my third-floor bedroom, carefully avoiding a squeaky step Barbara had warned me about. The following morning at the family breakfast, before leaving for church, Canon Cook sternly said, "The next time you come in late, step on the damn squeaky step near the first landing. Don't you understand that I can't sleep until everyone is home?" To me, the no-nonsense Canon had given me both a blast and a hug. These were good times.

When my voice changed, I auditioned for the Lyres Club, which was not the typical glee club in constant search for male singers. In the annual auditions, choir director Sam made sure to choose the best-looking girls in school and, like bees to honey, even the super jocks of the football and basketball teams auditioned. Membership became a status symbol as our girlfriends wore our club sweaters and pins. The system worked for me.

It was a long-standing tradition that the Lyres Club had an annual reciprocal exchange that culminated in a joint concert with another school. With an invitation from Concord, Maine, and not enough money to cover the costs of the charter bus, I volunteered to lead our first chocolate bar drive. Sales were slow, but I came up with the idea of selling the bars by consignment to every student at stations set up in the cafeteria and at every exit of the school. The campaign was a huge success and a valuable experience for me. I learned the value of teamwork, how to manage a committee, and the power of creative problem solving. I also discovered that if I had any lingering career ambitions in the fields of accounting or finance, they should be abandoned.

By the time I reached Grade 12, I was in the Lyres Club, senior band, a 16-piece dance band, Dixieland band, a barbershop quartet called the H2SO-Four (we loved chemistry), and, if that wasn't enough, the reserve navy band of HMCS Carleton. My final year of high school (Grade 13 in Ontario, at the time) was tough. The combination of academic studies, extracurricular activities, and a six-day-a-week part-time job at a florist forced me to let go of something and, sadly, I left the St. Luke's choir. The highlight of my Glebe years was the last annual concert where I performed in six acts, including singing my first solo ballad. At the final assembly before graduation, I received the trophy for outstanding achievement in contributing to the Glebe spirit. It went well with my sandcastle trophy.

Upon graduation, with not enough money for university or college, my identity tied up with music and art, and a guidance counselor's advice that I consider a career in social work, I had no idea where I was going. I had no direction and no driving passion for anything. All I wanted was a job and the ability to be self-supporting while I saved and pondered my future. I continued to work at the florist and a grocery store and eventually landed a contract with Crawley Films, an Academy Award-winning studio in Ottawa. Crawley's was producing a TV series, Tales of the Wizard of Oz, and needed grunts to work in the animation department. Innocently thinking that my cartooning skill might launch a career, I applied, was hired, and discovered my job was painting acetate frames, the equivalent of paint-by-numbers. Above my workstation were small bottles of gouache paint with labels such as "Pant Blue" and "Hat Red." It was boring. Relief came in the form of meeting senior animators from California on their occasional visits, terrific guys who shared stories of working with Walt Disney and Hanna-Barbera.

Having completed the contract, I was back on the street in need of a more interesting and better paying job. I applied to be a telephone installer for Bell Canada. After taking the required aptitude test, I was told I did not conform to Bell's selection criteria, though they wished me success in any future endeavors. I eventually got a job at the Department of Agriculture's Experimental Farm in Ottawa. Leaving music and art behind, I cut grass, weeded the ornamental garden, and harvested tobacco.

Sometime during this period, I became aware of the Ontario College of Art (OCA) in Toronto, which I hadn't heard of before. I found the college offered courses in industrial design, a field I had become interested in mainly because of my drawing. Through much of my early school career, I drew futuristic cars on the cardboard inserts used by the laundry for packing freshly starched shirts. My attraction to industrial design was also fed by an interest in three-dimensional objects, plastics, materials, and their form detail. Such things increasingly intrigued me as "modern design" emerged in appliances, furniture, and home entertainment during the late fifties and early sixties. Beyond form and function, I discovered the tactile dimension. I loved the look and feel of products that created a new intimacy between the product and the user.

With nothing to lose, enough money, and almost an understanding of what I might like to do, I put together a portfolio of high school stuff, cartoons, car designs, and drawings from the National Gallery and applied to OCA. Coming from an academic stream and competing with students from schools specializing in gifted students in art and design, I wasn't optimistic, so my acceptance was a delightful surprise. I packed my worldly belongings in an antique steamer trunk and left my hometown by train for the first time.

On Canon Cook's recommendation, I applied for residence at Knox College at the University of Toronto, a small Presbyterian college with a declining number of seminarians located on the main campus and a short walk to OCA. Enlightened for the time, Knox had opened the all-male residence to multi-faith and multidisciplinary influences and to everyone from freshmen to post-doctoral students. The building was a beautiful example of English Gothic architecture, with the three-story residence, a leaded-glass cloister with an open courtyard, cathedral ceiling dining hall, and a magnificent chapel and library.

Like Harry Potter entering Hogwarts for the first time (on a miniature scale and without the wizards), I moved in with the assistance of a residence host who helped carry my trunk across the courtyard to the freight elevator. Arriving on the third floor, he gave me the room key and left. Not knowing a single soul in Toronto, I was overwhelmed by a wave of loneliness. While staring into the beautiful courtyard below, it sank in deeply that my life had changed forever. It was a memorable, slightly traumatic moment, but I recognized that the only choice was to go forward. I was in control of my own destiny. My journey had begun and I was going to have fun.

The journey was interrupted when to my shock what I thought was my closet door opened and a giant entered my room. I later learned that renovations to the residence involved closing off the hallway door to the next room, leaving the occupant's only possible entrance through mine. For the next year, the guy next door would need to come and go through my room to take a shower or use the can. The blonde, six-foot-six giant was Jim Bee, the son of English Baptist missionaries. He had grown up in rural Jamaica and had come to Canada also to study industrial design. From that day forward, we were always seen together, especially since we moved often four times a day between what seemed to be two very separate worlds.

We walked from the Gothic elegance of Knox to OCA, a newly expanded complex, around the corner from the Art Gallery of Ontario, that could have been mistaken for a three-story high school or a shabby old office building with a newer building attached. Its only endearing features were the lovely Grange Park it shared with the Art Gallery and an internal concrete courtyard formed by the joining of the old and new buildings. The combined cafeteria and auditorium offered lousy food and a lousy place to meet. By contrast, Knox still maintained the traditions of 19th-century Oxford and Cambridge. We wore academic gowns for breakfast, lunch, and dinner, spilling, by tradition, as much food as possible in the annual quest for who could make a gown stand on its own. We sat at oak benches and tables and rose to attention as the dean and faculty entered and made their way to the elevated high table. Following grace, the "maids" on staff—who treated us as their sons and cleaned our rooms and made our beds—served our meals. It was a tough life.

The intellectual atmosphere of each world was similarly a study in contrasts, especially as these were the early-to-mid-sixties, the years of the British invasion of the Beatles and Rolling Stones, assassinations of John Kennedy and Malcolm X, early feminism, flag debates, civil rights marches, and a general questioning of just about everything. Living in the two worlds felt like getting two degrees for the price of one. I loved it.

Knox was a playground of intellectual engagement and healthy jousting and debate. I was living with residents in studies as diverse as theology, arts and humanities, law, medicine, engineering, geology, history, and philosophy. Surrounded by a cloister filled with a dynamic mix of socialists and capitalists, theologians and atheists, engagement wasn't a problem. At OCA, the swirling social currents generated discussion about artistic expression, psychedelics, advertising, Andy Warhol, pop art, and existentialism, though student interaction was limited. OCA's program was structured around departments—drawing and painting, sculpture, advertising and illustration, industrial design, etc.— and the building was physically structured around each department's needs. Such partitioning naturally impaired interaction.

Industrial design students were considered eccentric artists at Knox and "plumbers" at OCA. Debate at Knox was analytical and linear while OCA debates tended toward conceptualization. Remembering Rudyard Kipling's "Oh, East is East, and West is West, and never the twain shall meet," I often wondered what could happen if I could bring them together in some form of mutual coexistence.

OCA, founded in 1876, was Canada's leading art college. Its programs were based on the classic method of the German Bauhaus School, founded in 1919, which brought together art and craft and established the modern era of architecture and industrial design. Every OCA student, whatever his desired field, had to endure the Bauhaus method's demanding "foundation year." The courses taught everything from colour theory to calligraphy, sculpting, metal craft, life drawing, art history, illustration, and textiles. To this day, I remember hand drawing parallel, vertical, horizontal, and diagonal lines with a 2b pencil for hours on end without a ruler. Worse, I spent late nights painting in tempera the entire Munsell colour wheel. Not content to simply teach us about the system created by Albert H. Munsell in the first decade of the 20th century or to explain colour space on the three-colour dimensions of hue—value (lightness) and chroma (color purity)—they made us draw and hand-paint the damn thing, using only the principal hues of red, yellow, green, blue, and purple, plus the grey scale from white to black. It seemed at the time to be faculty revenge for being forced to endure first-year students. I later realized they were teaching us visual literacy.

With the foundation year complete, I had to apply to my preferred department. The dean and faculty reviewed first-year portfolios and selected 20-plus students for the three-year industrial design program. Besides academic achievement, they took prior art college education, additional interests, and age into consideration. As a result, the class included mature students who had studied engineering and architecture, a commercial photographer, and others trained as machinists and pattern makers. The mix also included a couple of married guys because the dean believed they were more mature and committed and would set the pace for the rest of us no-good party animals. He was right. Fortunately for us, there were no women in our class for distraction.

While I served as the industrial design class president, a few of us decided to create a new organization, the Association of Student Industrial Designers (ASID). After quietly negotiating with faculty and staff, we officially informed our department head that we intended to ask for a seat on the board of the Association of Chartered Industrial Designers/Ontario (ACID). The department chairman at the time, Charles Wetmore, was delighted that his students were finally showing some spunk and said, "What took you so long?" He took our proposal to the board and the members granted us one seat. Not bad for a bunch of students in a young profession that probably then numbered less than a hundred practicing professionals in all of Canada.

Charlie Wetmore was smart, demanding, and laid back, with a dark sense of humour. An advocate of a system design

17

pedagogy based on creative problem solving, he imposed a "problem-solution-benefit" structure to every project. Each came with a brief that described the scope of the opportunity, specific constraints, and scheduled faculty (read client) reviews during the life of the project. Through the design process, I learned a valuable discipline that would serve me throughout my career.

Almost every project assignment was a product that drew from other courses, from something as mundane as a built-in metal medicine cabinet to designing and building chess set pieces without the stereotypical icons of crowns, horseheads, and bishops' mitres. In the case of the medicine cabinet, the professor didn't give a damn about the industrial design and made us turn in the often-beautiful renderings and working drawings. As a result, most of the class, including me, got an F because the product was not manufacturable. To add insult to injury, the work was returned with dramatic oversized corrections in bright red marker (Munsell number 5R).

As I worked through various assignments, I began to discover the passion and values that would define my career and shape my quest for professional fulfillment. Everything was now about product, supported by courses that enhanced the focus such as ideation, materials, creative problem solving, drafting (working drawings), descriptive geometry, mechanics, history of design, and design research. I loved it all.

My favourite course, available only in the graduation year, was professional practice on Friday afternoon, geared to employment in the "real world." Charlie pontificated on his own client experiences, great and terrible, and on how to build professional presentations and client trust. More often than not, the class retired to the seedy Beverly Hotel bar down the street where Charlie was at his best. A fellow student once asked him the profound Zen-like question, "What is the secret of success?" Following a few moments of deep contemplation—and with a straight face—he replied,

"The secret of success is recognizing that your top dresser drawer only holds six shirts." Confused, the student said, "I don't understand." Without missing a beat, Charlie replied, "My son, if you don't understand, then you will never find success." We all laughed. For some reason, the question stayed with me. I guess I hoped the answer would be revealed by experiences gathered during a life's long journey.

Of the 20-plus students who started the industrial design program with me, 16 graduated and are listed among the college's most successful alumnae. For myself, I graduated filled with confidence and youthful innocence ready to take on the world whenever and wherever I might find a world I wanted to take on. I did not try to get a job with a consulting design office, which was the conventional practice. I wanted to enter the world on my own terms, not as a back-office gopher.

I gained experience working briefly with clients such as GE Plastics, Westclox, and Clairtone Industries. For GE Plastics, I helped a couple of their clients in the design of a handle and some kind of transparent cover. It was a dull job, but I learned a few things from their engineers. Westclox needed a design for the dashboard clock for American Motors' Rambler Ambassador intended for U.S. diplomats in countries with right-hand-drive. Rambler needed to remake the dashboard because the air-conditioning wouldn't fit under the dashboard with a right-hand wheel and, as a result, neither would the clock. The solution was a new shallow clock from Westclox with my design of a new clock face. The job took two months.

Clairtone was making quite an impact in those years with its TVs and home stereo products. I was involved in the design of Clairtone's stereos, the furniture consoles we called "coffins," and with the design of the front "mask"—the plastic front that surrounded the picture tube and contained the controls and corporate graphics—for their 13-inch black-and-white TV. The day I presented my design, which reflected Clairtone's image of design elegance and quality, I was joined in the conference room by retailer Mel "Badboy" Lastman, who smoked a huge cigar and said, "Gimme more chrome and wood grain. My customers love chrome." The job involved some fun and good learning, but I discovered they were playing off consultants, with each of us refining the others' work. Outraged by their ethics, I walked away and never bothered submitting a final invoice.

I discovered that I hated last-minute trivial rescue work and fixing others' mistakes. I could do it but didn't like it. I wanted to design products beginning with first concepts. I wanted to work within the problem-solution-benefit system that had captured my imagination. I had no idea where to find such work, so I went to the library and took out Scott's Directories of all Canadian manufacturers and looked for companies I thought could use an industrial designer.

One outfit back in my hometown looked interesting. An old Montreal-based firm, Northern Electric, had been building a research-and-development (R&D) campus in Ottawa. On a trip back home, I decided to pay the company a visit. Carrying my black 36x24-inch portfolio case, I approached the front desk and asked if I could see someone from personnel. Offered an application form, I told the very nice woman that I didn't fill out application forms and wasn't there for a job anyway. I was there to interview the company for future reference. Puzzled, she called the personnel office and asked me to take a seat.

In a few minutes, I met my first Northern executive. Dr. Bonnie Jackson, the director of personnel, invited me to his office. He was curious about the message he'd received and asked what I meant by future reference. I told him I was interviewing prospective companies to see if they could effectively exploit the skills of an industrial designer because, as a relatively young discipline in Canada, the profession was unfamiliar to many. He told me he knew what an industrial designer was, had discussed it recently, and, if I would like a cup of coffee, he would invite a fellow executive, mechanical engineer David Stevenson, to join us.

I presented my portfolio and discovered that Dave had been strongly advocating hiring an industrial designer since the company didn't then have one. He asked about my expectations for a starting salary. Caught off-guard, I suggested some number I vaguely remembered from the Association of Professional Engineers guidelines. Leaving my address, phone number, very thin resume, and references behind, I left delighted with the encounter. A week or so later, to my utter amazement, I received a job offer with a salary 15 percent higher than the number I'd suggested.

Much to my later surprise, it turned out that on that beautiful spring day in 1966 I had found my place. I had found a home and my quest for personal fulfillment had begun.

2 DISCOVERING A PASSION

Beyond what I learned from Scott's Directories and a couple of brochures I received with the job offer, all I knew about Northern Electric was that it made telephones and other equipment for telephone companies. Assigned to the outside plant department, I still had no idea what they did except they obviously didn't do it inside. But I soon discovered that it was already an old Canadian company, dating back to 1895 as the manufacturing subsidiary of Bell Canada in the earliest days of the telecommunications industry.

I learned that, over the years, the corporate structure evolved and for the first half of the 20th century Northern was partially owned by Western Electric, the subsidiary of AT&T in the U.S., and had access to technology developed by Western's renowned research organization, Bell Labs. Northern Electric operated much like a branch plant, manufacturing Western Electric products for Canada, though it did have a small research-and-development (R&D) staff of its own. Then, in 1956, Western Electric signed a consent decree with the U.S. Department of Justice in which it agreed to give up its interest in Northern. Bell Canada acquired most of Western Electric's interest in Northern Electric in 1957 and by 1964 owned 100 percent of the stock.

The question for Bell was what to do with this new wholly owned subsidiary, especially since it no longer had any patent and licensing relationship to Western's American technology. The consent decree gave Northern only 10 years of grace for licensed manufacturing, and the company had virtually no products of its own. There were many who thought selling it was the way to go, but Bell's president, Robert C. Scrivener, had a different idea.

From my earliest days with the company, I became aware that Scrivener was considered the visionary, the one who saw the opportunity for Northern if it could learn to stand on its own feet, free from Western Electric. He recognized the need to innovate or perish. He stepped up the company's R&D work with a lab at the company's manufacturing plant in Belleville, Ontario, in 1957. Other labs emerged at other plants in Montreal, London, and Brampton.

In 1959, Bell's management established an R&D headquarters for a new organization: Northern Electric Research and Development Laboratories. Ottawa was chosen as the new location of the lab because of its central location, the city's quality of life, the presence of two respected universities, and several government research organizations including the National Research Council, and the R&D section of the Department of Defence.

By the time I arrived, the Ottawa lab housed a few hundred people on a beautiful campus in the west end of the city. Seeded by core resources from its manufacturing centres and regional labs, Northern was actively recruiting innovators and administrators from all across Canada, the U.S., and Europe.

As neither an engineer nor a scientist and, thus, a stranger in the strange land of R&D, my new world seemed in many ways surreal. It was a Dilbert cartoon strip before its time, a place of white lab coats, ties with clips, and pocket organizers. Being the first industrial designer hired by Northern, I had no one to coach me on how quickly I would encounter the "pinstripes," a metaphor I adopted to describe executive management and other bigwigs and featured as cartoons in my lab books and journals over the course of my career.

Not long after arriving for my new job, I discovered what would become typical of the R&D spirit. Dave Stevenson had experienced considerable resistance in hiring the company's first industrial designer and applied a rule that I would use on many occasions throughout my career: Forgiveness is easier to get than permission.

The Ottawa campus struck me as a clear statement of confidence in the potential of the company. The administration building had a theatre with seating for 250 and outstanding acoustics designed by employee Bob Tanner, an internationally recognized acoustic engineer. It had a beautiful library with skylights and a professional staff worthy of any university. The administration building was joined by two glass-walled breezeways that led to two labs. Together, they shared a lovely courtyard with picnic tables. Impressive as the facility was, it was nothing compared to the people. There was a contagious vitality and a can-do team spirit everywhere. Even as a new employee, I could sense a feeling of destiny.

I was welcomed with ease, with one awkward exception. The illustration department filed a complaint during my first week. While recognizing my position as an industrial designer, they said I could do whatever I wanted provided that I didn't use colour. To me, that was an employment deal-breaker. The following day, awkward turned to hilarious when Dave got a call from the director of purchasing. She was unable to process my purchase order for coloured pencils because, by corporate policy, red and green were restricted to the accounting department. Purchasing even had a hierarchy to represent different levels of seniority. I wondered how the illustrators could get by without colours. Fortunately, the issues were resolved in my first meeting with Brewer Hunt, the first vice president of the R&D organization, who agreed with my position. I later enjoyed a great working relationship with the illustrators and accountants. I also took great pleasure in signing purchase orders in red.

To my delight, I discovered that Northern Electric was not new to research and development, and had quite a reputation for its own innovations. I discovered the company had once manufactured Hammond organs, and, with a patent generated during World War II, a series of Baby Champ desktop radios with miniature vacuum tubes. Its Dominion Sound division designed and installed the entire video switching system for the CBS broadcasting centre in New York. It developed satellite and antenna equipment and provided Hughes Aircraft with the electronics for Canada's ANIK satellite. Out from under the influence of Western Electric, there was an underlying strength and passion to take on the world.

I felt ready to take on the world too, but my first assignment was not very challenging: a sheet metal cabinet for a product I can't even remember. Much more interesting was a project in support of community service. Bell Canada had a long tradition of such service, especially aiding the hearing impaired and the visually impaired. The Montreal Rehabilitation Institute asked Bell to help in the design of artificial arms for children born without limbs because their pregnant mothers took the drug thalidomide. Bell referred the request to Northern's R&D centre and Dave Stevenson's outside plant group accepted the challenge.

Dave had a captive model shop within his lab and there I met Helmut Lucas, a brilliant machinist from Germany. I was asked to provide industrial design to his efforts but his skills were without equal and he needed little help from me. To create prosthetic electro-mechanical arms for a four-year-old girl, he needed to build miniature parts and, with nothing commercially available to build them, had built his own milling machine. His hydraulic pumps were so precise that no one could initially build them to the tolerance that would avoid leaks. My only contribution was suggesting that rather than building hands to the effective two-finger and thumb "claw" configuration, he should create a full hand because all handicapped children wished to look normal to their friends.

Together, we researched and found soft materials used in flexible toy dolls and he created flesh-colored, fully articulated, covered hands. Helmut, Dave, and I went to Montreal and met Claire, a beautiful and fun-loving little girl. Fulfillment came in watching her joy as she was introduced to her class. Later, based on feedback from the doctors, Helmut had to create a slip clutch for the fingers and wrist because if Claire were mad at classmates she could pinch their nose and rotate her prosthetic hand beyond 180 degrees.

Working with Helmut and Dave's team, I learned a new work method based on longstanding research processes and procedures. Engineers and researchers used lab books like diaries. The books were standard equipment for everyone and every page was printed with a place for date, signature, and witness. They were considered so important that when a book was filled, it was filed in the library. I picked up the habit and discovered the real value when applying for my first patent. The lab book emerged from the academic environment with its focus on documenting research to be published in juried scientific journals, but was also critical to documenting the first date of witnessed disclosure and patent application—the famous example of disclosure timing being Alexander Graham Bell beating Elisha Gray to the patent office by a day or two.

My lab book evolved into a daily diary that I took to every meeting. It always served me well, though in later years my books played a role in two controversial issues. One book was subpoenaed because I had been working with Dictaphone on a joint development product to create an answering machine for our modular SL-1 business phones. Unknown to me and to Dictaphone's staff, pending a possible corporate acquisition by Northern, the company was in the process of due diligence to confirm all material facts in regard to a sale or purchase. The deal fell apart when it was discovered that the wife of Northern's CEO at the time, John

Lobb, inadvertently bought Dictaphone stock during the due diligence process. On the second occasion, my book was subpoenaed in a trademark infringement case. While we won the case, my notes, entered into evidence, also included candid expletives and an associated cartoon of the division general manager. Fortunately, he thought it was funny and asked for a personal copy.

Dave Stevenson soon sent me to meet with Lloyd Armstrong, the director of the regional lab in London, Ontario, who Dave had spoken to in his quest for agreement on hiring an industrial designer. The lab was part of the plant that manufactured Western Electric telephones under license, with its work centered on the transfer of product from Western for cost reduction and manufacturing efficiency. Challenged with a new Western phone that featured a dial in the handset, the London guys were trying to reduce the cost of the handset and the base by using existing components. The result was bulky and ugly. Lloyd came to me for help, bringing along a rough balsa-wood model made in his lab. He uttered the words that would launch my first product, "See what you can do and if, in the process, you can come up with a better idea we'd love to see it."

My professional practice course at OCA taught that we should always give the client what they ask for first, so I set out to make a silk purse out of the sow's ear Lloyd had given me. Working with the outside plant group was a blessing. I worked with great mechanical engineers. I could do so-called working drawings but had trouble dimensioning them for transfer to the pattern makers with their milling machine requirements. Bill Moss, a manager with a Masters degree in mechanical engineering, spent days teaching me to draw critical cross-sections. In spite of it all, the guys in the shop still needed to make hand-made cutters for my inspired signature detail of tapered radii.

Engaging the staff in our terrific model shop, we built a model of my design that met the requirements of cost avoidance and using existing components. Most who saw the model found it acceptable, but no matter what I tried, to me it was still a giant bar of soap. Since I had Lloyd's permission to come up with a better idea, I set out to design a completely new alternative.

I researched the anthropometric dimensions of human hands, ear-to-mouth, and cheek clearance. With only personal experience in using a phone, I decided to go out in the field to observe how they were installed, where they were placed, and how they were used and abused and serviced. I spent a week in Guelph, Ontario, with Bell's residential installers. To say the experience was enlightening is a gross understatement. It was a wonderful opportunity to be with people who loved their jobs and took pride in customer satisfaction.

I learned a lot about their frustrations that in many cases were ignored by management. Given the customers' right to change their minds about colour and location, the truck carried six premium colours in addition to basic black for both desk and wall versions of the telephone set. While I stapled line cords to baseboards and observed customers, I watched the installer go back and forth to the truck. If he didn't have the choice in inventory, we waited for another truck or taxi to bring the item from the field office. In those days, second visits were a last resort.

I talked to a lot of homeowners. I discovered they were willing to pay a monthly premium for colour because they wanted the phone to integrate well with their personal taste and decor. I discovered that if they wanted a desk set for the bedroom and a wall set for the kitchen, they often changed their minds during the installation by walking around the various rooms to verify a choice.

Armed with new insights and a feeling that management wasn't as knowledgeable as they might appear or think themselves to be, I went back to the drawing board and into frequent management consultations. In one meeting, I asked, "What about the living room?" I was struck by the odd comment from a Bell marketing guy who replied, "Don't bother. Our research says nobody wants them there." True, I hadn't seen many phones in living rooms, but perhaps that was because no one had ever offered them one.

The next few months were great fun, filled with ideations (sketches) and the challenge to fit the damn components. I worked long nights and occasional 24-hour days and shared many, many ideas with colleagues. I used the date-signature-witness process for drawings that showed the most promise and filled more than one lab book.

To work with the London engineers, I took my first ever airline flight ("white knuckle" doesn't do justice to the twin-engine Viscount turboprop trip hopping from Ottawa to Toronto, and on to London). I showed the London group early comparative models and was able to convince them that several components and the ringer size were the real problems. After a few days of back and forth, we reached a series of acceptable solutions. They agreed that a two-gong ringer could be replaced with the smaller single-gong version used in the hated Princess phone. A smart engineer concerned with sound quality later modified the gong brass alloy, sweetening the sound and reducing the clatter.

I made regular visits to London as the development progressed, and finally went there for a complete design review. The engineers proudly presented a mock-up made with temporary prototype tooling. I was shocked. In an obvious collision of values, my new colleagues had implemented dozens of small changes in the interest of mechanical packaging and tool design, believing that the changes did not violate the industrial design intent. I discovered the error in my ways. I had failed to understand the need to track changes in the collaborative design process.

Asked what I thought, while thinking my design had turned into a complete piece of shit, I diplomatically declared the prototype completely unacceptable. Following a very short and awkward discussion in which I tried to describe the loss of the intimate visual and tactile details critical to the whole product experience, lab director Lloyd Armstrong called a coffee break and invited me to his office. He declared that the product would not proceed without my sign-off, in spite of any schedule delays, and asked if I was prepared to spend all my time in London. I agreed and we returned to the conference room where the development project was stopped.

I commuted to London for the next few months, working in a new off-limits lab constructed for the whole team. I discovered the proof of the adage "innovation is ten percent inspiration and ninety percent perspiration." I knew I would only get what I deserved unless I had the passion to champion the product's integrity from prototype development to market launch, including marketing.

It was a terrific learning experience for all involved. I learned about tool making, plastics, manufacturing, and assembly while they learned about the industrial design process. An accomplished mechanical engineer responsible for many of the prototype's changes once referred back to the meeting that stopped the product and asked how I could see the differences. I explained that as an industrial designer I had been trained to a high degree of visual literacy and could detect details much smaller than 50 thousands of an inch. Taking out the original drawings and measuring their mock-up, he accepted my answer with grace and a smile, and that evening took me sailing.

As the design work was going on, I was also researching colour with Professor Ed Carswell of the University of Toronto's architecture faculty, an expert in colour psychology. He hand mixed colours and painted four-inch plastic wall tiles and we spent endless, delightful hours exploring the range. It felt like a graduate course. Ed was a wonderful man with the nurturing nature of a grandfather. He was a great storyteller and would later accompany me to executive presentations, always to the great delight of the audience.

Because Northern was a subsidiary of Bell Canada, all products to be deployed in the Bell system were controlled by the systems engineering group in their labs. The director, Jim

Kennedy, would become a great coach and friend. Working with his assigned engineering manager, we would later need to take the approval process through Northern and Bell management simultaneously, which also provided a great learning experience.

As the product approached final design, I was encouraged to keep it confidential and under wraps because of patentable features. I designed a presentation black box that featured a black acrylic cover and fitted walnut base. I always covered it in dramatic style with a black cloth during my presentation for a magical final reveal. As awareness rose through the ranks, people started talking about the magic black box and cloth.

As I was getting ready to take the product up the executive management chain, I experienced for the first time the politics of power and control. The new product was to be discussed at a senior management meeting to which I was not invited. I was asked for the model and my presentation slides. I refused. I said I valued any first-hand feedback and discussion and added that until the design was authorized or rejected for manufacture by Northern and Bell, it was attached to my hip. Where it went, I went.

Northern Electric's president, Vernon Marquez, graciously invited me to present the product to the board of directors for final approval and, because the parent company would also be the largest customer, Bell Canada's board had to approve too. Accordingly, I became the first non-manager to present to the presidents and boards of directors of both corporations. For a 25-year old-designer, that was a lot of pinstripes. I was introduced to the hallowed inner sanctum of the board's floor at Bell Canada's headquarters and at Northern Electric's—only blocks apart. Both were beyond anything I had imagined. My lasting memory was their opulence and isolation from the streets below. That journey introduced me to Robert Scrivener, the guiding spirit behind Northern's development and the very image of a pinstripe. I remember so well his dark suits, white shirt, striped ties, and starched white breast-pocket handkerchief. This, of course, was standard issue for businessmen at the time, but Scrivener pulled off the uniform with a distinct flair and quiet panache.

In my presentation, I had fun with a slide show that included a background problem statement, field research and analysis, colour research, a wide range of concepts explored, and solution-benefits to the consumer, supplier, and manufacturer. Nowhere did I show the final product in any photograph. For my grand finale, I dramatically removed the cloth and opened the box. What I had named Contempra was born.

The first phone to be designed and manufactured in Canada since Alexander Graham Bell's, Contempra featured a dial in the handset, nine colours, and, in an industry first, a patented combined desk and wall set that required no modification for installation, a little innovation that reduced inventory by half. Learning from my field research with Bell installers, I was able to sell the new colours and increase the choice from five to nine based on reduced truck inventory (no need to carry separate products for desk and wall), and the value of customer choice. Unable to predict product mix prior to launch, I used the early production theft rate from the London plant. The workers loved the product and that metric proved to be remarkably accurate.

I had only one small barrier to overcome before launch. Unknown to me, Bell had created an employee-naming contest for the phone. This being 1967, Canada's Centennial year, they thought it would be appropriate to tie the event and the product together. Unfortunately, someone forgot to tell the left hand what the right hand was doing. I had already created the name and sold it as part of the decision process. I had no choice but to ask to attend the committee review. Caught between a rock and a hard-place, I needed to diplomatically rationalize Contempra while somehow supporting their initiative at the same time. It wasn't easy.

The top of their list included Tinker Bell (yikes) and ExpoPhone. Much to my relief, I convinced them that the name needed to work in both official languages, be gender-neutral (no Tinker Bell or Princess), and present an image that was, oh, say, contemporary. Thankfully, they found a creative way to award prizes to the employee contestants without ever naming the first-prize winner.

Contempra also launched me into the rather exciting world of marketing and sales. I needed to help Northern sell the phone to other Canadian telephone companies, and to American companies independent of AT&T. I had insisted on designing the logo for the product I named, defining the packaging, and dealing with Bell's ad agency at the time, McCann/Erickson's Canadian head office in Montreal. The agency's executive VP of creative was an amazing guy and took me under his wing.

Swept up in the momentum following my first press conference in Ottawa, I was suddenly on the road. Not that long since my first white-knuckle flight, I was now on the corporate jet crisscrossing the continent in what felt like a concert tour of North America. I was visiting customer headquarters and doing television, radio, and newspaper interviews, all the while never quite understanding how the innovation of a little telephone could generate such a fuss.

The experience introduced me to the power of relationships in marketing and sales. I was met at every stop by our regional sales executive and soon discovered that some of them actually had an office on their customer's premises. One customer described the relationship to me as, "Jim is part of the family. The only difference is that he gets his paycheque from Northern." Many of our own sales executives had started their careers with customers, installing Northern Electric equipment.

Hugely successful, Contempra eventually sold millions of units in 15 countries. It was exhibited in New York's Museum of Modern Art, the National Galley of Canada, and the U.K. National Design Center. Bell Canada's annual report actually listed Contempra's success as a contribution to positive earnings.

To me, in addition to increased demand for industrial design and the personal pride and accomplishment of seeing our product come to market, fulfillment came from proving that innovation creates new wealth, careers, and employment enriches the local community at every level. It was an insight for me to discover that invention leads to a passion for innovation, not the other way around.

I discovered that innovators are demotivated by conventional corporate policy and practice. Their motivation is based on being empowered with the freedom to explore. Their adrenalin will surge to the challenge when hearing "it can't be done." Typically, innovators have disdain for bureaucracy, meetings, human resources, and undue process. They understand R&D is collaborative and will fight any corporate process that encourages internal inertia. Ideas are not patentable. It's only the embodiment of the idea that can be patented and they are experts at incubating ideas and creating embodiments. If necessary, they will simply slip work "under the bench," jargon for "we'll keep it going no matter what others say."

In my experience, innovators are the strongest group in the corporate sub-culture. Driven by passion and facing resistance, they will always apply the rule: Forgiveness is easier to get than permission. One innovator summed it up, "I love this job so much, but my paycheque is always a surprise. I just keep going and hope that somewhere out there somebody is opening a cheque from a customer that reads "payable to Northern Electric." Thank God." I often shared the same thought.

It took me until my second year of art college to confirm that I wanted to be an industrial designer, and another four years to discover the passion. It was worth the wait. Not content with product styling, I loved beginning with original concepts and exploring the whole product opportunity. I had the opportunity to develop a new product from first principles and to shepherd my creation from conception to production and into the market. I thrived in the culture of collaboration. It was exhilarating. Innovation was in my blood.

3 CREATING AN IDENTITY

Contempra was important to the image of Northern Electric's R&D organization and its growing reputation, but it was far from being indicative of all the activity underway. In the mid-1960s, the labs had successfully launched SA-1, a mini-bar community dial office switch designed for small U.S. towns that was very successful and established Northern's reputation in an overlooked market.

Around the time I joined the company, about a dozen researchers began working on a stored program switch system, the SP-1, reflecting the then controversial belief of engineers at both Bell and Northern that digital switching—basically controlling networks with computer code—would be a cost-effective way of improving switching performance. The SP-1 project was the lab's biggest investment to that time, a multimillion-dollar R&D gamble with a huge payoff. Designed to compete against AT&T in smaller telephone company markets, the switch went into service in 1969. It was ideal for rural independent operating companies and won Northern a major beachhead in the U.S. It also introduced the company to advanced micro-circuitry and software design and development. The SP-1 became a huge success throughout North America for years to come.

The labs were already fully engaged in the next leap of innovation. Computer-controlled switches were technologically challenging, given the limitations of the early days of computing. There were few industry-standard integrated circuits, so in 1969 Northern built a state-of-the art facility across the road from the Ottawa labs to fabricate components. There, they established Microsystems International, to create the microprocessors required to move to a digital world.

The labs were hotbeds of activity, growing to more than 800 people by 1968. The company was aggressively recruiting, especially in Europe, bringing in some Brits who would later become friends and well-known players in the industry, including Colin Beaumont, Ian Craig, Mike Cowpland, Terry Mathews, and Peter Luff. Dr. Graham Sadler, another Brit who retired as president of Northern Telecom Electronics, told me one of his priorities on his recruitment drives in London was finding new players for the Ottawa Beavers, a local rugby club he had founded. He needed more players to expand the league. During interviews, following the review of candidates' resumes and academic credentials, he always asked, "Do you play rugby?" Many did, and went on to found the Twin Elm Rugby Club.

Recruitment was made easier by the labs' growing profile and reputation, helped along by *Telesis*, our own journal created in the late 1960s as a counterpoint to the *Bell Labs Record*, the gold standard for technical journals. Solely generated within the Northern Electric Research and Development Division, the journal's aim was to portray R&D progress in telecommunications to the scientific community, government, and customers, particularly Bell Canada. I participated from the beginning, writing articles and helping the staff recruit a graphic designer.

Concurrent with my work in product development, I found myself exploring the broader implications of digital technology, which was clearly a massive technical discontinuity. I began to extrapolate where the market would be from the perspective of value to the user. Were there societal implications of the convergence of voice and data in a digital network? I was invited to present a paper at the "Telecommunications and the Arts" conference in 1970, sponsored by the Canadian Department of Communications, the Secretary of State, and York University. Just a few years after being told that I was not Bell material, I was both amused and proud to share the stage with Robert Scrivener, now Bell Canada's president.

My paper was titled "Telephone and associated technology as a future instrument both for the production of works of art and as a distributor of works of art." It was theoretical in nature and described what was, in effect, a hyper-publishing system encompassing all other systems. To avoid burdening the text with the expressions "the system" and "the model," I simply called my theoretical system Alexander. To quote from the paper, Alexander was "at once a publisher, an agent, and a distributor, it is an electronic entrepreneur seeking out participants and linking them to suppliers. Self-updating, it will make its own yellow pages. Shakespeare, the chemistry of platinum, the art of cooking rice, or the elements of telemetry will become listings in the telephone book. Alexander brings together, as complementary and reciprocal, the functions of the telephone, television, computers, and libraries. It is also reciprocal to the extent that it allows exchange between itself and the user." The paper went on to describe how Alexander would compress time and space and accelerate access.

The ideas presented were simply an extrapolation of social norms. The conference was held about a year after the U.S. government issued a request for proposal for what would eventually become the Internet, but it would take until the late eighties and early nineties before the true capabilities of digital networking technologies could be commercialized and widely appreciated.

Scrivener spoke on the same topic, though unfortunately his speech has been lost to history. All I remember is feeling that I was just a featherweight who had designed a telephone, yet here I was on the podium with the conference heavyweight. Thinking about the roughly twelve layers of management between us was sobering. I kept thinking that the big difference in our presentations was that I was still the only industrial designer on Northern's staff while he was actually in a position to bring our complementary digital visions to life.

Lower down the food chain, I was fully engaged in telecommunications R&D, working on SP-1 equipment packaging, the attendant console for the digital Pulse private branch exchange (PBX), the extremely rugged Centurion payphone, and the Venture operators headset, with the world's first patented electret noise-cancelling microphone. Later in 1970, after learning that I couldn't manage all product demands myself, I recruited three industrial designers, my first hire being my university alter ego, Jim Bee.

I was promoted to manager, sending me off on an adventure I had never imagined or planned for. Most of my management experience came from trial and error and a couple of courses in organizational development. My first real challenge was learning to design with my hands in my pockets. I had to learn how to empower. If in frustration, I asked the designers to move over at the drawing table and then showed them what I wanted, I would get what I asked for and would have deserved nothing more. Hands in my pockets meant hands off and allowing their individual creativity to explore the opportunity. This was easier said than done. It took me a long while to appreciate that successful working relationships were based on reciprocal loyalty and trust. Reciprocal loyalty and trust are the foundation of any great corporate culture, large or small. They are the reason employees love what they do and where they do it. That learning meant a great deal when I later ventured out of my comfort zone and rose through the management ranks.

Loyalty, trust, and a collaborative effort were also hallmarks of the SP-1 development, which required close cooperation between Northern Electric's R&D and manufacturing divisions and Bell's engineers who had to make the switches work in the unforgiving operating system environment. The collaboration was so successful that Bell's management decided to merge the separate R&D divisions of Bell and Northern to create an independent R&D subsidiary—70 percent owned by Bell and 30 percent by Northern Electric. Creating a new subsidiary marked a major strategic redirection for both companies and was the first critical step in Robert Scrivener's plan to make Northern a major player in the telecommunications industry. The timing couldn't have been better.

Northern reached outside of Canada to find a leader for the new subsidiary, repatriating Donald A. Chisholm from the U.S. to become vice president of the new R&D division in 1969. Chisholm, with a doctorate in physics from the University of Toronto, became a senior scientist with Bell Labs and director of electron devices. Back in 1968, he was appointed managing director of Bellcom Incorporated, a Western Electric subsidiary involved in system engineering the Apollo space project and the post-Apollo manned space program.

We first met in my tiny one-man studio (so small I had to step outside to change my mind). I was surprised to see his beard and casual dress. Beards in our R&D community would later be dated BC (Before Chisholm) or AD (After Don). For the record, mine was BC.

Shortly after his arrival, he asked me to redesign his corner office on what was called teak row. Maintaining the only endearing feature—a complete back wall of teak storage and bookshelves—the task was easy and fun and done in one simple discussion. I needed no catalogue or drawing because Don knew about every product and manufacturer I suggested. Changing only the furniture and painting the ceiling dark brown, I tossed the large mahogany desk and replaced it with a small teak roll-top desk made by Herman Miller, with two leather Eames chairs placed in front of the desk. Instead of traditional sofas, I selected four low-slung brown leather chairs from Knoll International, placing a large clear glass and stainless steel Knoll coffee table in the center. While attending a meeting there, I discovered Don, with his feet on the table, had holes in the bottom of his penny loafers. He secretly loved nurturing the image of the eccentric scientist.

Don was a product guy and researcher and loved being around the people and culture of innovation. Never one to direct, he listened, loved intellectual debate, and searched for consensus. He was famous for his walkabouts, simply wandering into an office or lab, joining the conversation, then typically leaving with a something-to-think-about question. The questions were always worth thinking about, disconcerting as they were for some staff.

He was fun to work with. A man of incredible intellect, he also was passionate about the history of cultures, architecture, the arts, and, of course, technology and innovation. An expert in calligraphy, he annotated memos with a fountain pen, always writing in lower case and never crossing a "t" or dotting an "i." A note signed in lower case—*dac*—could launch a project. As the recipient of many *dacs*, I tried to figure out the length of reply required, adding up his words and using the same number in reply, minus one. The *dacs* became shorter. My final one word reply was "why?" He answered "because." True to form, he had figured out the game. Damn.

Don was charged in his new role to consider a name and identity for the new subsidiary. This was mission critical for him and he decided early on that their development would be orchestrated and funded internally. He asked me to participate in defining both the identity and the vision of the new entity, an opportunity I happily seized. On my journey from the breadth and depth of Contempra to exploring the implications of digital technology, I discovered early on that vision and leadership matter. Vision implied more than just words to an industrial designer. Vision involved a visual manifestation that embodied the spirit and values of the organization. The opportunity to translate a vision into reality at the birth of an organization rarely comes along.

I was still working for David Stevenson in outside plant and, thanks to him, doing what I wanted, where I wanted, but Dave was always happy to nurture and never stepped in the way. As far as he was concerned, I'd work directly with Don on the launch of the new company and call on whatever resources I needed to get the job done.

With that I set off on an amazing trip of discovery. Little did I imagine the gauntlet of approvals that lay ahead. Deciding on the name came relatively easily, at least to us. The first non-contentious name we discussed, considered almost too obvious, was Northern Electric, Research and Development, Company Limited. Don found it dull, conveying nothing more than a change from a division to a subsidiary, and asked me to create new criteria. After playing around with names such as Innovation Canada and Innova, I brought back a simple list of relatively pragmatic objectives. I thought the name should honour parentage and product. Parentage: Bell and Northern. The product: Research. As simple as that, we named it Bell-Northern Research, later to be reduced to the familiar BNR.

Requiring the approval of both Northern Electric and Bell, we experienced the first resistance from Northern's board of directors because we were eliminating the word "electric." Bell Canada's board included Madame Pauline Vanier, widow of the former governor-general, and she insisted that the word Canada be included. Other board members from both companies added the word development. As only two independent board committees could accomplish, the name that emerged required a whole line of copy and a deep breath to read in either official language: Bell Canada, Northern Electric, Research and Development Company, Limited.

Don could not stop grinning when he came back from the meeting where the name was handed down and tried to give me the news. Outrage and laughter ensued. What to do? Switchboard operators had to answer our phones, so we decided to simulate and record their calls for playback to both boards. We asked operators to say "good morning" or "afternoon" and the name of the company in English and French. One operator couldn't do it despite three attempts and we left all her attempts on the tape. We then repeated the exercise with, "Good morning. Bell Northern Research." Armed with a high-quality reel-to-reel tape recorder, Don and I went to appeal our case to the boards of both companies. To our relief, they accepted our "compromise" and we got our name.

With the name in place, we addressed the graphic design challenge of the corporate identity. To that point, we hadn't come up with any concepts. From my design unit, I enlisted Jim Bee, John Mahan, and Richard St. John, a recent OCA graduate working his first job, to join me in shaping the image, values, and attitudes of the new entity.

Prior to Don's arrival, the labs were steeped in traditions that put me in mind of robed meals at the Knox high table. Business cards featured academic achievements. Formality ruled the dress codes of researchers and scientists (white lab coats), technical staff (brown), and management (suits), though the wilder management guys would occasionally remove their jackets. Don was the antithesis of a pinstripe. He was more at home wearing a tired grey cardigan sweater. He was interested in transforming the culture from a rather stuffy technology centre into something more akin to a research campus passionately pursuing product innovation and knowledge, a place of ferment, exploration, discussion, and debate. We agreed that the spirit and vision of the new company should address everything and challenge convention.

Our challenge as designers was to translate the spirit and vision into a visual language and icon. Our design studio had restricted access, and the development proceeded on a need-to-know basis. As a result, my design team and I spent many wonderful hours with Don, discussing everything from new product, to art and philosophy.

The Bell-Northern Research logo was our greatest passion. To us, it was not just a logo. To us, it was heraldry. It was an icon graphically conveying the spirit and vision of the company and its employees. As it evolved, we were concerned with how it would scale in the multiplicity of applications from small business cards to a mighty roadside plinth. We created a visual graphic equation to show the evolution and meaning of the icon. We chose three symbols to spell out our goal and found a way to combine them to create a company signature that we believed would be intuitively understandable everywhere. The first was a simple stick-figure representation of humanity commonly used since prehistoric times. The second was the world, which represented our environment. The last was an arrow, a universal sign for direction.

With that in front of us, I translated it back into a word statement that would become BNR's vision: "People, reaching out to the challenge of bringing the world together, all in the spirit of innovation, dedication, and excellence." Don approved. The carefully considered words were not exclusive to researchers. The vision was inclusive, inviting everyone's commitment to an exciting future. It stood the test of time, becoming the spirit of the entire corporation twenty-six years later, with only a single word—"leadership"—added, appropriately enough because the market at that time had clearly assigned leadership.

Next up was the colour, Northern and Bell both used blue. Following lots of testing, we decided to ignore the convention of primary colours for corporate identity and chose purple as our corporate colour, rationalizing it as the colour of heraldry and knowledge. Over the next 25 yeas, BNR's R&D staff throughout the world became known as "purple people," a testimony to the fact that vision and leadership matter.

Faced with a launch date the first day after the Christmas-New Year's break in 1971, absolutely everything had to be produced and ready to go. The logo design naturally led the way, followed by the business cards, corporate signage, and stationery from forms, to labels, to technical report covers, to vehicles and boxes. Hitting tradition straight on, we eliminated academic degrees on business cards for everyone, simply using the name and position. Leading the way would be the new president of BNR. In spite of being known affectionately as Dr. Don, his card would simply read: Donald A. Chisholm, President. (At Don's retirement party years later, Bob Ferchat, a former Northern president, presented Don with a long, multi-fold business card featuring all his degrees and honourary doctorates that reached almost to the floor.)

Remembering an innovator's comment, "I love this job so much, but my paycheque is always a surprise," we decided as a design feature to address the most personal document employees ever received in those days: their paycheques. Passionately pursuing every detail, we discovered that cheque suppliers had never been asked to apply any graphic corporate identity. They just printed a company's name in their standard typeface. Working with purchasing and payroll, we rejected numerous suppliers before finding the right one.

Everything began to fit into place. Faced with replacing the existing roadway entrance sign to the main campus, we grappled with construction schedules and discovered we needed to hire an architect. At 30x40 feet and one piece, the base of the sign needed to be a cofferdam to accommodate building codes for hurricane force winds and earthquakes. Unable to determine the size of the font or icon for legibility on the high-speed road, we created a large concept sample on cardboard using the letters "North" of Northern. Jim Bee and I drove back and forth while our student industrial designer held up the sign. Thinking he was hitchhiking north, two drivers stopped and offered him a lift. The student was convinced he was the victim of our prank, though it was just a hilarious accident.

The sign was at least a hundred feet back from the very long curve on the main road, so it didn't need to be parallel to the campus entrance road. Standing at the location with our architect, he told me the plans would require a survey of the exact location for construction specification. In what happens when you put two mischievous designers together, he suggested that, given its unveiling on the day the new corporation was to be announced, just for fun we should use magnetic north to align the sign. I loved the idea. Charting the bearings for the exact day, he added it to the working drawings. The children of the area would later call the landmark sign "The Big Purple Book." Completely flood-lit from the base with halogen light, at night it seemed translucent, magically floating in space. Forty years later, I have no idea how far magnetic north has moved, but the sign is still there, though now, sadly, repurposed.

With everything in production, we began working on the formal introduction to the media and employees, to take place in the central lab's auditorium. Loaded with the latest technology of 1971—Kodak carousel projectors and a dissolve unit—we wrote and designed the launch presentation for Don's formal announcement. Since designers never leave well enough alone, we were also determined to use the special one-time moment to convey the spirit and vision of BNR. The resulting audio-visual production, our first, used the template of the graphic design equation as the non-verbal script, with the presentation based on the reveal of the iconic logo. Richard St. John spent weeks extensively photographing lab buildings, products, and employees in various cities. From hundreds of slides scattered across a simple light-table, we composed and edited a four-minute presentation we felt conveyed the spirit of our new organization.

Then came the real challenge. We needed to use six projectors and the Kodak system worked for only two projectors and one dissolve unit. We had no ability to synchronize an audio track. So we improvised. We placed three pairs of projectors on top of the auditorium projection booth and three dissolve units inside, with very long remote control cords. Using our high quality, reel-to-reel tape recorder and our soundtrack from the band Blood Sweat and Tears (honestly), we hooked the deck up to the auditorium's outstanding sound system. One problem remained. Lacking the technology to connect and program three dissolve units and a soundtrack, we decided to be a three-headed human program system. All we needed to do was to start the music and, armed with a remote control in each hand, simply wing it. Amazingly, after a number of rehearsals, Jim, John, and I discovered that the three of us could actually finish at the same time. Unable to fit in the projection booth, we stood to the sides and behind the audiences. This was going to be a live show.

Chisholm could be unpredictable, so we went into stealth mode with his wife, Marilyn, and executive assistant, Edith, to make sure he was properly attired for the big event. Never knowing what he would wear, we bought a purple dress shirt and tie for the occasion. Sure enough, we later learned he had come down for breakfast in a green suit and to sharp words from Marilyn, saying, "You're not wearing that to the office today." He changed into a dark grey suit. Arriving in his office, Edith presented him with the shirt and tie. The jacket didn't last long.

Addressing the assembled employees and media, Don, as always, was terrific, speaking in his usual conversational style about what we would accomplish together, then introducing the slide presentation, which he hadn't seen. He knew what we were up to, but conveyed complete trust and wanted to see it for the first time at the event with all the other employees.

The launch went off without a hitch. Even us three amigos ended on the same beat. Don told me at the end of the day that a young engineer had come up to him at the end of the launch with tears in his eyes, saying he was upset with the multi-screen presentation. Don asked why and he replied that no corporation should try to touch the innermost feeling of an employee. Don suggested that the presentation was meant to tap into our shared values and that, having just seen it with everyone else for the first time, he shared the young engineer's feelings. I took it as a fine compliment.

Over the next few weeks, we packed everything into a newly painted BNR station wagon and took the show on the road, visiting every lab in Montreal, Belleville, Brampton, and London. We planned the tour around Don's schedule and he joined up with us, fulfilling a promise he made at the launch to visit every lab. Don wore his purple shirt, sans jacket and tie, and after his brief speech and the A/V presentation, everybody joined in for coffee and cake (with purple icing, the beginning of a long celebratory tradition). Don then went on a walkabout to meet the staff.

People from every location recognized themselves and their colleagues in the presentation and everyone bought into the values presented. The response was wonderfully positive. Given the years the labs had been operating successfully as a division, the transition to a wholly owned subsidiary was seen as a natural progression. The name, corporate identity, and values were new, but there was not a single management or organizational change associated with the launch.

There was, however, a big change in outlook, purpose, and direction. We may not have foreseen that we had just given birth to what would become one of the most innovative and widely respected research-and-development organizations in the world. But we knew that under

Chisholm's leadership, the purple people of BNR had the passion and potential to make communications history.

While working with Chisholm on the launch of BNR, I scribbled in my lab book: "Without reach, there is no challenge. Without risk, there is no reward. Without vision, there is no future." True to this day, it applies to every company and to any entrepreneurial start-up. Without vision, there is no future.

4 SHAPING A NEW WORLD

Thanks to the vision of Robert Scrivener, Northern Electric had a bright, exciting future. He offered a challenge to Northern and created the opportunity by having an R&D lab staffed with the young upstarts who saw the industry discontinuity in the conversion from analog to digital technology.

Being fully committed to digital technology was a provocative stance at the time. The industry wasn't sold on the idea. Bell Labs had developed the first partially digital switch but were having difficulties capitalizing on the opportunity. As the 1970s unfolded, the Bell Labs people badmouthed the technology in papers and at conferences, even while they were still working feverishly on it. They knew digital systems had the potential to revolutionize communications, but they risked falling the proverbial one-step-behind, and likely decided that the best defense was to discount the capability altogether. Lots of people in the industry agreed and suggested that Northern continue manufacturing analog switches since digital switches would be far too expensive.

Northern ignored such conventional business wisdom and decided to take a leap of faith, betting the business on the belief that the conventional wisdom was wrong. Northern was right. The evolution of the digital switch over the next decade would mark the transition to an entirely ncw world of communications.

Establishing BNR and delivering it into the capable hands of Don Chisholm was just the first stage of the company's ambitious project to create a full line of digital switching and transmission products. Don's genius and laid-back style nurtured an *esprit de corps* among the staff and generated endless streams of creative thought as teams started work on a broad range of innovative technologies and products.

In its start-up phase, BNR was funded by corporate headquarters, but that changed as the new company got up and running. Each division of Northern Electric contributed to BNR's budget and Don rightly feared that development rather than pure research would eventually consume all available R&D resources. An excellent manager, Chisholm knew what would happen if he didn't control the long-term integrity of advanced technologies. With the R&D program under the control of the divisions and, therefore, subject to the pressures of short-term expediency, he negotiated for a separate 15 percent research fund also to be paid for by the operating divisions. Thus was born BNR's famous Capability Fund, which was his way of ensuring BNR stayed out front in technology development.

To ensure it never became a slush fund, researchers were held to account with objectives, milestones, deliverables, and regular reviews. But given the fund's limited budget, the application process was made as simple as possible, compared to the arduous process for the rest of the program. The biggest differences were the right to take risks, and the right to fail.

The annual highlight was Capability Day, with an event held in the auditorium attended by senior Northern executives, divisional general managers, and the executive management of BNR. Lab visits followed the presentations.

Researchers spent many long nights preparing for the big event. Being forced to make a presentation to 250 people and working to the event deadline resulted in many long nights of testing lab results, dry running slide shows and, later, PowerPoint presentations.

Researching optoelectronics, the advanced technology group entered the field of lasers and demonstrated fiber-optic transmission. Over the years, I recall seeing the first prototypes of optical scanners, fax machines, and a colour digital movie camera. I witnessed the development of our own computer communications email system and the delivery of movies on demand through the network. Early on, I remember a smiling Northern VP, David Vice, a driving force behind the company's research efforts, sitting in the front row at advanced presentations saying, "I always thought you guys were nuts, but do you have any idea how much bandwidth that would consume?" Little did he know that was just the beginning. Over time, the Capability Fund produced a significant portfolio of patents.

As BNR grew, I decided to change the name of my industrial design unit to Design Interpretive (DI), a name I invented to embrace the whole product value. I also decided to engage in some still necessary educational work among people both outside and inside the company about what the design unit provided. Many people still thought of an industrial designer as someone who just took a product that was already constructed, played around with the outside shape to make it look nice, then put it in a good-looking package. While engaged in our lab work, we also tried to spread the word that design provided a crucial and key link between the customer, and the technical and manufacturing staffs.

In an article in BNR's journal *Telesis*, we got across the idea that the designer's job was to translate the philosophical to the tangible, to identify a problem, express it in manageable terms, and come to an optimal solution. To do that, the designer had to absorb all kinds of information about all aspects of the intended product and its use because really effective design, then and now, combines knowing the past, knowing what kinds of things are changing around you, identifying a gap in the market, and throwing a creative solution into it. It integrates the technological and manufacturing aspects of a product with the less tangible demands of the evolving communities in which the product is used. Until the designer's been through that process, the design can't mature in his mind.

The article laid out the view that turning a complicated problem into a simple one can't happen without going through a two-stage conditioning process, being analytical, scientific, and methodical in approach in the first stage, and synthesizing, imaginative, unconventional, and freethinking in the second. The essence of the design exercise, it said, was to discover, understand, and assimilate all the different requirements for the product and then to suggest an overall conception, which would reduce all this complexity to one simple statement. This constituted the transition from philosophy to tangible product. We made our case firmly and often, and appreciation for industrial design gradually grew.

We were fortunate in our situation at BNR. Designers then (and even now) were often not brought in early enough in the product-development process. But we were involved at the very beginning in terms of strategies and helping to define and direct the services we'd like to develop. At BNR, the designer became a complementary member of a multidisciplinary team forging a strategic link between the consumer and technology. Close interaction generated mutual confidence and trust, without which we would have failed.

As the labs expanded to meet demand, my little group was pressured to relocate. Seizing the opportunity, we moved to an old one-room schoolhouse across the road from the lab main entrance. Leased from the federal government's National Capital Commission, it had been used by the HR department for management development courses. Too small to fit our prototype lab and its new state-of-the-art five-axis milling machine, we added a portable schoolroom at the back and joined it with an enclosed bridge that contained our coffee bar.

As designers, we had to have some fun and put our personal touch on everything. The teacher's tiny office became the boardroom and we used beanbag chairs for seating. Not surprisingly, the beanbag chairs became handy beds on far too many long nights and would later become synonymous with visits to our conference rooms in other locations. Guests would sink into the chairs to watch presentations which we had to start by going into the furnace room, turning on our Kodak projector, installing the slide tray, and pointing the lens through the hole we punched in the furnace room wall.

We removed the teacher's door and replaced it with two narrow ones that opened into the boardroom, the doors being covered with a black-and-white wallpaper called "Secretarial Pool" featuring a parody on Renaissance etchings of topless women (these being days long before politically correct gender sensitivity). In one final act of renovation, while maintaining one cubicle for a women's washroom, we refused to change the boys' washroom, leaving the child-height urinals, which led to memorable visits and discussions. Concerned that out of sight could become out of mind, we pledged to always have lunch across the road with the lab people and bought a folding bike to expedite our trips. We designed stick-on labels for the large internal mail envelopes used for daily pick-up, with the label featuring the word "schoolhouse" and a stylized apple, though without a bite out of it as a more famous apple came to have a decade or so later.

With more work than we could handle, a 40-hour, five-day week was pure fantasy. But it didn't matter because we were infected by the passion of the people across the road. They loved what they did and loved coming to work every day or night. Personally, I too was infected with their natural sense of collaboration, and it didn't matter if it was with a physicist or Edna in the cafeteria who, seeing you in line for breakfast, had it ready by the time you reached her. There was a sense of family and life in our schoolhouse, and it was fun. Freedom reigned, empowerment prevailed, and about the only way to get into trouble was withholding your opinion or hiding the truth. What you thought mattered and, no matter how junior, if you were hesitant you could expect someone to ask, "What do you think?"

Trust, I learned, is mission critical to collaboration. Without it, a subculture will develop and take innovation underground. Trust is so easy to lose and so hard to get back. Fortunately, that was not the case during our digital revolution. Trust and collaboration were so natural they were rarely discussed. Amazingly, in spite of its size and growth, BNR felt and acted like a start-up. It was an exciting place to be.

We had to stay on our toes, especially when Scrivener implemented the second stage of his long-term vision. BNR may have been bubbling with creative innovators chomping at the bit to take on the world, but Northern was still just a relatively small Canadian company with a rather stodgy manufacturing sensibility. The Canadian market couldn't possibly generate the revenues needed to fund the research required to build a new digital world. To rectify that situation, just five months after BNR officially opened its doors, Scrivener gave Northern Electric a new president.

John Lobb, a lawyer and finance expert, had been an executive vice-president at International Telephone and Telegraph (ITT) and a disciple of the famous Geneen School of Management (named for Harold Geneen, an American businessman most famous for turning ITT into a giant multinational conglomerate). The Geneen style was driven by a tough business plan discipline. Lobb had a reputation as an ass-kicking businessman and he delivered on it in spades. He was charming when he wanted to be, but could be brutal in an operations review, which some called an inquisition. He was an indefatigable road warrior, constantly on the move between the company's operations. He worked as hard as he expected others to, and hammered away at reducing costs and driving greater efficiencies across the board.

He was never a product guy and considered R&D an expense rather than an investment. He had no affinity for innovation or research types, other than as walking opportunities for cost reduction. During Lobb's tenure, a lot of product innovation and advanced technology stayed below the bench. Thankfully, passion prevailed at BNR even as we adjusted to a regime of fiscal restraint.

Lobb was a tough taskmaster and his mission was to prepare the company for expansion beyond its traditional market, to shape it up, and take it public. He knew how to do it. In terms of vision, he was once asked what business he was in and replied, "We're in the business of making money." While not a very inspirational vision, it was at least honest and direct.

My first encounter with him, other than during lab tours and visits, came when he became frustrated with the London plant's slow pace in its transition from electromechanical to fully electronic components. He directed the head of the Microsystems International division to challenge them with a totally new product. Working with the division, I designed a very small dial-in-handset product named Avanti, still one of my favourite pieces of work. We created a working prototype clearly directed as a wake-up call. Ready to go, we prepared to take it to one of Lobb's executive operations reviews as ordered.

I travelled to Montreal on a Friday with my boss, Jim Kyles. We took our seats behind the grand executive table and waited for Lobb to enter and take his place at the head, surrounded on both sides by his senior executives in descending order. Lobb was known for his light stomach, and inside intelligence warned me to watch for his use of antacids during the meeting. I noticed he was chewing antacids when he came in. Not a good sign. My presentation was to be followed by a review of the advanced technology components. In the middle of my presentation, he stopped the meeting and launched into a tirade about the value of money and how this show was wasting his time. He demanded to know who was responsible for putting this presentation on the agenda, apparently forgetting that he himself had asked for it. The room became very quiet. Feeling the need for a quiet theatrical exit, I mumbled an expletive under my breath and tossed a pencil on the exquisite mahogany table. It bounced on its eraser and hit Lobb in the head, who stormed out of the room, his entourage in tow.

With the meeting cleared of everyone but the presenters, Jim said, "I guess that didn't go very well." The drive back to Ottawa was quietly tense. When I arrived at the office on Monday, I was intercepted at the security desk and asked to go directly to the BNR president's office. Don Chisholm did not invite me to take a seat. Informed of the Friday meeting, he assured me of his continued support and confidence and quickly dispatched me to my boss's office next door. I felt that I'd been sent to the principal's office and then directed to the vice-principal for discipline. Jim simply said it was time for me to lie low. He noted that I had eight weeks of unused vacation, which was against corporate policy, so I was on a one-month vacation effective the next Monday. He asked me to see him on Friday and tell him where I was going. I left pissed-off, but then spent a few days reflecting on my position. As instructed, I returned to Jim's office and told him that I was off to Greece to visit the Oracle of Delphi. After some good-natured discussion, Jim said, "Good-bye. And keep the receipts."

Lobb didn't hold a grudge. Some time later, when I was working late into the night with a few colleagues in Boston, he dropped into the small boardroom there to ask what we were up to. In a good mood (he wasn't chewing antacids), he offered us a beer and took us to the nearby kitchen. The fridge was locked with a chain looped between the handles, but he said someone would come by with the key. That night we met Mario (with key in hand), Lobb's chauffeur and rumored bodyguard, an impeccably dressed, charming, almost stereotypical Italian. Before he left, we knew the best nearby Italian restaurant for dinner and discovered Lobb's favorite beer: the fridge was full of Labatt's Blue.

In 1972, Lobb opened the first Northern plant in the U.S. in Port Huron, Michigan, just down the highway from our London operation. During his time as president, he created a U.S. corporate subsidiary, opened a head office in Boston, and split his time between Boston and Montreal. He later moved the U.S head office from Boston to Nashville, Tennessee, which was a much better hub for all the travel involved in his job and, it was rumoured, a shorter commute to his Florida condo.

By the time he left the main company in 1976, Northern had been radically changed. Bell Canada had reduced its ownership from 100 percent to 80 percent. It was a public company listed on the New York Stock Exchange. The deadwood had been cleared out of the manufacturing-oriented, inward-looking old firm. The company had a substantial presence and saw growing revenues in the United States and had expanded into Europe, Asia, and the Caribbean. Revenues and profits soared year after year. All CEOs are strong characters more powerful than any corporate identity or marketing and advertising campaign. Their values have an impact on the very spirit of all employees. With Lobb, sadly, fear and second-guessing had become embedded in the corporate culture.

In my group, we were up to our ears in the design of a new line of business terminals and were trying to understand the switching and transmission product lines. With our regional labs in Belleville and London, we created a new line of business telephones for the SL-1 private branch exchange (PBX).

The SP-1 introduced in 1969 had a computer-based electronic control system, but the switching matrix was still electromechanical. The SL-1 was fully digital in both control and switching, the world's first all-digital PBX aimed at medium-sized businesses. Named Logic Series, the line featured desk and wall mounting and an Amphenol connector bus for attaching modules without additional wiring. Installers and telecom managers loved it because for the first time a speakerphone could be installed by simply plugging it into the phone set. We used the experience from colour research on Contempra and reduced manufacturing and customer inventory by creating snap-in faceplates. With one standard colour—beige—the faceplates were also available in black, brown, green, blue, and purple. We waited for others to observe the remarkable similarity to BNR purple. A little mystery now and then can create folklore. The terminal portfolio provided the customer interface with what would become the world's most successful fully digital PBX.

We then plunged into the world of the central office, the nerve centre of every telephone company's network. It was all new to us and we reeled from industrial designer culture shock as we explored everything from sheet metal to huge rack-mounted bays of equipment. BNR even built a captive office and gained permission from the regulators to research and test the products on the live network. A senior lab executive said to me with just a hint of mischief, "It's a good thing they think we know what we're doing." The captive office would later feature full software upgrades as downloads to customer networks worldwide—something unheard of at the time.

The Pulse PBX, the first fully electronic switch, hit the market by late 1972 and the SL-1 had its debut in 1975. The labs continued extending the technology to the central office with digital multiplex switches (DMS) for delivery by the end of the decade—the DMS-10 for small central offices and the

DMS-100 (capable of handling up to 100,000 telephone lines) for large ones. Don Chisholm's baby, the DMS-100 was one of the most influential inventions in Northern's history and a major source of revenue for more than 15 years. By fully integrating switching and transmission, the DMS family changed the way telecom systems were built. By the mid 1970s, BNR-designed products accounted for around three-quarters of Northern's sales, compared to less than 10 percent in the 1960s.

During this time, I met the head of BNR's engineering team, Colin Beaumont, and Northern's chief corporate strategist, Derek Davies, both brilliant Brits whose contributions to the company's success cannot be overstated.

Colin, often described as the chief architect and champion of all things digital, did not suffer fools lightly and was tenacious in his defence of the technology and product. He loved a pint at a local pub, had a dry, almost cynical wit, and had a team that would have gladly thrown themselves on swords or other sharp objects in his defense. They had passion and commitment and loved the freedom he gave them to get on with the job. He was in charge of the SL-1 development.

Derek, who arrived via ITT, was a pinstripe and, by nature, very private. He understood product and marketing and was convinced that the market discontinuity of the product under development was being underestimated and understated. He championed the idea of Northern stepping out in front of the competition technologically, and in terms of the American market, promised early delivery dates for the digital switches.

That idea met with substantial resistance. The manufacturing plants were barely able to meet customer demands for the SP-1 and Pulse PBX, and thought promising a future leap into a new technological realm was nuts. Demand exceeded supply, so why would anyone in their right mind obsolete their own product? There is only one answer.

You must have a vision of where the market will be and go there. If you don't, someone else will.

In a daring move, Derek took out an ad in the trade press early in 1976 announcing, "Northern is in the midst of the most ambitious digital switching program ever undertaken. We want you to be part of it." Coincident with the ad, Northern Electric changed its name to the now more accurate, Northern Telecom.

Derek knew that creating an event with an immovable date was the best way to turn a ship this size. The company was challenge-driven and would continue to be so for decades, and nothing sharpens a challenge like a publicly declared marketing event. The event, a seminar to be held at Disney World in Florida at the end of the year, was eventually named Digital World, a registered trademark then, and now a generic term.

To spread the word among the North American telephone companies in advance of the seminar, Scrivener appointed his executive vice-president of operations at Bell, Walter F. Light, as president of Northern, with John Lobb becoming chairman. Walter was the ultimate product guy. With 25 years experience in Bell Canada, he loved the business, the customers, the technology, and the culture. He also knew a great deal about Northern product.

Walter's passion and enthusiasm were contagious, especially in contrast to the former regime. A first-class operations executive, he also understood employee motivation and the unstoppable power available if people believed in themselves and had the self-confidence to rise to a challenge. He was charming, candid, and often not very diplomatic. GOYA—get off your ass—was an acronym attributed to him and used throughout the company. Under Walter's leadership over the next ten years, product innovation took hold and Northern's reputation as an industry leader grew around the world.

Because of my product contributions to the digital initiative and my experience in launching BNR, I was invited to contribute to the market positioning of Digital World, by helping with product photographs and the presentation material. The build-up to the announcement marked the first time I participated in such a large collaborative multi-divisional customer event that went far beyond my experience with the design and launch of Contempra. For the first time, I heard the term 'bet the business' used by a Northern executive.

Anxiety continued spreading throughout the company right up to the seminar. There was concern that the announcement would not only obsolete our current product, but cause our customers to defer procurement and wait for the new range of switches. Beyond the market risk, the event could also be career limiting to the lead innovators and their teams who staked their careers on an advanced technology and being first to market. Without collaboration and extensive team spirit, we could have never pulled it off.

The seminar threw our competitors into turmoil. Not only did we gain new customers, those customers told our supplier competitors that if they weren't ready to be totally digital, they would slow down their network upgrades and wait for Northern products. The other shock at Disney World was the appearance of a new chairman and CEO of Northern Telecom, Robert Scrivener, as Lobb moved on to head the rapidly expanding U.S. subsidiary. It came as quite a shock to the Canadian establishment and to industry watchers around the world that he left Bell for Northern. The media and the chattering classes speculated about a demotion, but he didn't think of his move that way. I think he found Bell boring and decided Northern was where the action was—the one place where he could realize his vision.

Digital World was a huge success and a testament to how a sleepy branch-plant manufacturing subsidiary can morph into a world-class powerhouse. It wasn't luck. Enlightened management saw opportunity and had a vision, but it required passion and commitment from everyone involved to realize it. As the saying goes, "You can't learn to sail until you leave the dock." Our Digital World products would revolutionize the telecommunications business and lay the foundations for a new and, eventually, web-based world.

We had no way to measure the level of market disruption and discontinuity that would result. But we were driven by passion and commitment, and for the next five years the labs became hotbeds of research, innovation, and product development. With the announced rollout dates of 1976 to 1980, the pressure dramatically increased. The DMS-10 entered the market in 1977 and the DMS-100 two years later.

Leaders must nurture the organization as a collaborative community, a combination of people, process, and product. Beginning with people, if they love what they do and the organization engages them with processes that respect their value and contribution, a reciprocal loyalty will emerge. Product is the metric of success, the heart of the organization, the face of the corporation. It makes the cash register ring. Together with an unrelenting focus on the future, there is no limit on what can be accomplished.

By now I had received an unheard of double promotion and was made a director, probably because I had successfully taken a function to a critical mass and was now considered a resident corporate expert. I had jumped in with both feet and was up to my neck. As a senior manager working across the product divisions, I began to see the implications of rapid growth. Internal operations, because they face in, will grow, impervious to market dynamics. In contrast, never free of speed bumps, the triad of people, process, and product is always vulnerable to everything from short-term expediency, to economic and/or market turmoil. By its very nature, the R&D process is dynamic and the people just want to get on with the task at hand. Too often, employees were forced to endure flavour-of-the-month business fads and experiments, poorly conceived processes that become more disruptive than constructive and created no new value.

Still feeling like a young pup without a day's formal management training, I was now one of the bureaucrats on the treadmill of annual operating plans, capital and expense budgets, and organizational development. My freedom to innovate came with an obligation to perpetually chase money. Fortunately, I was surrounded by the collective wisdom of executive coaches who nurtured my development while I bumbled and stumbled, and who understood how important it was to know when to let me fall on my face without harm. They coached me through dangerous situations with limited injury. I recall their comments about my tendency to not suffer fools lightly and the need to acquire a little patience. Damn, this was hard work. But I always seemed to find my way to wise counsel.

At the end of the 1970s, when Robert Scrivener was Northern's chairman and CEO, I managed to hitchhike a flight on his corporate jet. I was in Nashville for meetings at the plant that manufactured residential terminals, meetings that were supposed to last a few days but finished much earlier than expected. In those days, connections were really terrible and I couldn't get a flight back to Ottawa until the next day. The executive assistant trying to get me a flight said she knew the corporate Gulfstream was in Memphis—Scrivener served on a number of corporate boards and was attending a board of directors meeting there—and would be flying back to Montreal. Corporate policy stated that, if no customer was on board, I could hitch a ride provided the executive who booked the flight approved. She suggested a call to our central flight office and, with approval, I could catch a commuter flight to Memphis and then another to Ottawa after arriving in Montreal. Once cleared, I headed to the Nashville airport and made it to Memphis with time to spare. Needless to say, I was already on board when Scrivener's limo pulled up to the plane at the private terminal, and had made sure with the captain that I wasn't sitting in his preferred seat. Ah, the nuances of corporate traditions.

Following the normal greetings, it was wheels up within minutes. When we were cleared to move about the cabin, he offered to make me a drink—rum and coke—and poured his own neat scotch. We settled down, he with his files and me trying to look busy by following his lead. Some time later, and out of the blue, he looked across the aisle and asked me to name the dollar amount at risk for me to delegate a meeting to a staff member. As a young director, I answered $50,000. Curious, I asked him the same question. To my shock, he answered $50 million. He considered his number in terms of his span of control and implied that that was a small number.

Taking on the tone and mode of a mentor, he went on to discuss the need to trust and empower if I aspired to rise in the management ranks, which I did, though not obsessively so. To him, trust and reciprocal integrity were the foundation of all business relationships. He talked about his own early lessons and about how easy it was to micro-manage, only to discover that the process restricted his own personal development as well as restricting his staff. Through empowering his staff, he liberated himself.

He suggested I needed to learn to manage the strategy and delegate the tactics, and went on to make a point I've never forgotten. As CEO, he owned the strategy and the vision, and considered the operating and marketing plans to be tactical. When I asked for his planning horizon, he answered 10 years. This was all pretty heady stuff coming from my chairman and CEO.

Later in the flight, he reminded me that I had met his nephew in Europe some years earlier and had shared the sunset with him at the Temple of Poseidon at Sounion, Greece. With a slight grin, he asked how I enjoyed the toke. When I asked him how he knew about that, he laughed and replied that he and his nephew were both history majors and he had heard all about his travels to the ancient world. I resisted the temptation to tell him that I was only in Greece as a result of my pencil incident with John Lobb. It was a relaxed, enlightening, and thoroughly enjoyable conversation.

When we arrived in Montreal, he gave me a warm good-bye and asked the captain to fly me to Ottawa. If only for 35 minutes, I got my own Gulfstream. This was a new world to me.

5 EXPANDING INFLUENCE

As the multi-year Digital World product rollout continued into the 1980s, the BNR labs entered a new stage of expansion, physically and in terms of influence within the industry. The push was on to consolidate the gains made in the American market since the Scrivener days when Northern Telecom's presence in the U.S. grew from five factories to 25, and the number of U.S. employees in all areas of the business—sales, manufacturing, administration, and R&D— expanded from under a thousand to more than 13,000.

R&D is always capital intensive, expensive, and has a long lead-time to market, independent of downstream manufacturing investment. By definition, R&D implies risk and is a clear signal of commitment to every employee, while hopefully sending a shudder through every competitor. It is transparent, is tracked by every analyst, and can be seen in every quarterly and annual report. At its peak, Northern was investing 15 percent of revenue in R&D. BNR Central began constructing three additional Ottawa labs and regional labs across Canada. The U.S. expanded alongside manufacturing plants to meet growing market demand. In the first half of the eighties, new labs opened up in Mountain View, California, and Research Triangle Park, North Carolina.

Back in Ottawa, certain that the future of communications was software-based, the company went on a hiring spree of software-capable people. Key advances had already been made by a separate company formed in 1977—Bell-Northern Software Research—that became our Toronto lab in 1981.

Even though I was not a software guy, BNSR's work sparked a renewed interest in office automation that dated back to my York University white paper from 1970. Some years earlier, a senior BNR scientist had introduced me to Bernard Muller-Thyme, a medievalist, philosopher, and, of all things, a management consultant who was an old friend of both Marshall McLuhan and Barrington Nevitt, an engineer, theorist, and frequent McLuhan co-author who once worked for Northern Electric. I became friends with Bernard and Barrington, pioneers at the forefront of identifying the societal implications of communications for how we would soon live and work. I enjoyed frequent visits with them, engaging in many hours of philosophical debate.

Those discussions complemented the work of the Toronto lab whose researchers were at the leading edge of qualifying and quantifying the impacts of office automation. Rather than addressing automation in purely technological terms, they were taking the user-centric view so dear to my heart. Through an extensive research program called Office Information Communications Systems (OICS), they influenced and became known as leaders of the evolving industry through numerous articles in *Telesis* and papers in academic journals. One of the frequent *Telesis* authors and a leader in our office automation research was Don Tapscott, a kindred soul first working in collaboration with Design Interpretive psychologists in Ottawa and later with the lab in Toronto. OICS formed the core of his 1985 book, *Office Automation: A User-Driven Method*, the first of 15 books that helped make Don one of the world's most influential thinkers on all things digital and an internationally recognized management authority on innovation, media, and the social and economic impact of technology.

With software becoming the *raison d'être* of almost everything, the Toronto lab researchers developed our internal email network COCOS (computer communications system) and new telephone features and services such as caller ID, voice mail, and call forwarding. Their work set benchmarks that other suppliers were forced to match.

In Ottawa, all the new hires put a lot of pressure on current and new facilities, especially at the company's Carling Avenue campus. Design Interpretive outgrew our schoolhouse and we graduated to a new leased location shared with the systems engineering division. Called Carling Square, it was 10km closer to downtown. With offices on the second floor and our prototype lab in the basement, we created a ping-pong room next to the lab, rationalizing it as unused space we could use to prevent lab staff isolation. During the approvals phase, seeing the layout drawings and the words ping-pong, the director of building facilities gave me a call. Concerned about setting precedents, he suggested I call the room "prototype storage" and, when ordering the table, call it a "folding table for layout and product photography." I agreed. It worked so well that we had tournaments with our friends in systems engineering.

Now upgraded with blackout blinds, a large electronic controlled screen, and a projection booth with editing suite, our conference room featured 20 beanbag chairs and a few director chairs for any who felt uncomfortable sitting on the floor. For me, the only drawback to the new office was that my home was only a 15-minute walk away, resulting in my spending more time at work, not less.

Design Interpretive set out in new directions, building on our experience and clear success that went beyond technology alone, which I believed could rarely provide a long-term competitive advantage. The real and sustainable market differentiator depended on the design of next-generation technologies that best matched the ways people actually processed and exchanged information.

I felt that increasing our understanding of the user and chooser experience was crucial to expanding our influence and impact on product design, and we took the first of three steps by integrating within DI a small human factors group already in existence in BNR that was initially ergonomic based. The second step added a behavioral research function and a research lab for usability testing. We also recruited people with advanced behavioural analytic skills from post-graduate psychology departments of Canadian universities, ground breaking at the time and, in some quarters, controversial. Over time, the skill base of our behavioural research group included more than a dozen PhDs in psychology. To complete the triad, we added technologists who allowed us to design the electronics and implement the whole product solution.

Certain that the future of communications was both software-based and user-centric, I nurtured and occasionally pushed the integration of multidisciplinary product teams. Some described this as trying to mix oil and water, but I likened it to gathering artists and eggheads in the same room. In the process, we extended our span of influence to include leading-edge market research methods. We also extended the long-standing relationship we had with our corporate magazine, *Telesis*, offering their art director a home with kindred spirits in DI. As a result, and with additional recruiting of graphic designers, we began to develop group expertise in graphic user interface (GUI), soon to be a critical development as personal computers came into the market.

Normal to any period of prolonged product development, I learned that people need a break from the day-to-day churn of work in progress. Fast projects with a short stimulus and quick response time can do the trick. I decided to follow the example of the famous Italian industrial designer, Ettore Sottsass, who closed his office completely for two days in frustration with his clients. He challenged his staff to design an airport terminal for butterflies. Living above his office, he sat on his balcony and determined the winner by counting the butterflies landing on the airport terminals placed in a park across the road.

With our office closed for two days and a commitment to not even answer phones, I challenged the staff to create multidisciplinary teams to design a series of residential phones for the retail market we were sure would come, though at that time phones were still owned by Bell and rented by the month. People were not allowed to plug their own phones into the network.

At the end of the first day, each team presented its initial concepts to everyone while management provided the pizza and beer. On the second day, supported with more pizza and beer, imagination prevailed, complemented by costumes and custom T-shirts that one team had designed and had somehow delivered to the office. One presentation featured "Honest John Blobb's (Lobb) Deep Discount Phone Store." Another featured the "So to Speak Teleboutique." The little experiment in group mental health was fun and successful. Oddly enough, years later we would design Teleboutique retail stores for Bell Canada and design a series of successful "Imagination" products featuring names such as Alexander Graham Plane, Kangaroo, Cubby, Dawn, and Doodle, offered in colours such as Pony Red, Benny Blue, and Germaine Green.

DI became recognized as a world-class centre of excellence by combining creative (approximate), research (analytical) skills, and technology (implementation). Its unique and leading edge competence was confirmed during a benchmark study sponsored by the American Design Management Institute that included in its sample corporations such as IBM, Texas Instruments, 3M, and GE. Years later, DI experts in industrial design and GUI would extend their careers as core competencies with Apple, RIM, Microsoft, and Nokia.

BNR as a whole had caught the world's attention with Digital World and was acquiring a higher profile and greater influence by contributing to a two-way flow of information within the industry. Throughout the 1970s, Don Chisholm hosted BNR events in Ottawa that included guest speakers such as Buckminster Fuller, Alvin Toffler, Vice-Admiral Joyce Hopper, and Sir Kenneth Clark. I contributed to the sharing of information by maintaining connections with old colleagues while discovering new friends such as George Nelson and Syd Mead along the way. I can't recall how we were first introduced, but both created opportunities both for me to break out and for them to bring their expertise into our circle. Ever the optimist and champion of design as the way things give meaning and relevance to the human experience, I invited George and Syd to Ottawa on separate occasions to speak to Ottawa's growing high-tech community.

George Nelson was an architect, industrial designer, and one of the founders of American Modernism. He had been head designer for Herman Miller, the American manufacturer of office furniture and seating, and later established George Nelson Associates. His clocks, tables, and furniture were world famous and part of the permanent collection at New York's Museum of Modern Art.

Through George's good friend Eliot Noyes, the head of industrial design at IBM, I was twice invited as an IBM Fellow to speak at the International Design Conference in Aspen, the predecessor of what is now the TED conference (Technology, Entertainment, Design). Held each spring, the conference was a rite of passage for young designers and students, who drove from across the continent and camped near the mountain springs, joining other attendees who included a who's who from America and around the world. During my second conference, I met Ettore Sottsass. Wearing a black hat and cape and resembling Salvador Dali, his talk, delivered with a very heavy Italian accent, was titled, "Blah, blah, blah... a day in the life of a designer." Chronicling his dealings with clients, he read his diary for the entire day, complete with all the expletives and frequent blah, blah, blahs. While we laughed, I think we all might have had one or more of those days.

George Nelson gave a fascinating and thought-provoking presentation in the BNR auditorium based on his 1977 book *How To See: Visual Adventures in a World God Never Made*. By popular demand, we had to add three additional performances.

Syd Mead had been an industrial designer with Ford Motors for many years and eventually branched out as consultant, design illustrator, and futurist. He later became the conceptual designer for science fiction films such as *Blade Runner*, *Aliens*, and the original *TRON*. When we were together, we loved to rant, rave, and laugh about the state of design and the world in general. It didn't serve any purpose, but was wonderful therapy.

I subcontracted Syd to work with me when I was contracted from BNR as a creative consultant to Disney Enterprises for the development of the Experimental Prototype Community of Tomorrow (Epcot) theme park to be built at Disney World in Florida. Walt had died back in 1966 and there was some confusion about his intentions for the park. The big question was whether the "C" meant community or communications. I was asked to address communications, which won the day, with a focus on technological innovation and the culture and cuisine of 11 nations.

Working there was a wonderful experience. All new employees and consultants had to attend Disney University on their first day at the park. On my day, I joined up with professional dancers, kids working in park restaurants, and a new VP of hospitality for Disney Hotels. These guys wrote the book about management training. Customers were "guests" and every employee was a "host." Using the language of theater, all actions were "good show" or "bad show." Walking through the theme park with a senior VP, I noticed he picked up a spilled ice cream without calling attention to a nearby maintenance worker. "Good show" meant it was his job, on the spot. I was impressed, especially when later that day he allowed me to go through the park dressed as Winnie the Pooh's pal Tigger. The work was terrific fun and my sojourn felt like a sabbatical. I still have some framed original Syd Mead sketches.

In Ottawa, Syd gave a presentation, sponsored by BNR, to the schools of architecture and industrial design at Carleton University based on his books *Sentinel* and *Dragon's Dream*. Free to students, the school amphitheater was filled to overcapacity and required a second presentation that afternoon. The spirit of enquiry and collaboration within our Ottawa community was liberating, energizing, and downright thrilling.

Nearing the end of the multi-year digital product roll out, Northern experienced a turbo boost not of its own making early in 1982. The AT&T Goliath agreed with U.S. courts to divest its regional Bell operating companies (known as BOCs or Baby Bells), the divestiture to take place two years down the road. AT&T would retain only its long distance business and its manufacturing subsidiary, Western Electric, to be renamed AT&T Technologies. Suddenly, the American switching market was wide open. The Baby Bells, long feeling that they were restricted to captive supply from AT&T, welcomed Northern with open arms. The opportunity of a second source of supply finally gave them price leverage. Within those two years, Northern was supplying 21 of the 22 U.S. operating companies.

This held out many new opportunities, though among businesses outside the telecommunications industry, Northern Telecom was still something of a mystery. But Walter Light had a vision of how telecommunications networks and the computer industry would eventually evolve into what he called the Intelligent Universe, a new realm where machines of all kinds would be able to connect with each other. But the digital revolution, in recognizing the convergence of voice and data, also introduced a rat's nest of proprietary operating systems and incompatible protocols and standards by multiple suppliers. This became a significant issue to both telecommunications companies and enterprise customers who didn't like having to get locked into one supplier.

Our vice-president of market development, Derek Davies, once again sensed an opportunity for Northern to reshape and help redefine the industry, moving the markers in a very competitive field. He thought it was important for Northern to be the first company to say it had customers' needs in mind and could assure them that they'd be able to connect equipment from all sorts of suppliers and the system would still work. Getting out in front on the issue would strengthen our preferred supplier status with current customers and make the company name more prominent among other enterprises in the U.S. and foreign markets. He convinced Walter to lead the charge on another customer seminar along the lines of Digital World, an event that would promise a solution to a pressing and growing problem, excite our customers, and catalyze and focus our R&D.

For reasons never explained to me, I was assigned to work with Eugene Lotochinski and Bob Dyer on the Intelligent Universe project. I knew of both executives, Canadians who worked out of our American subsidiary in Nashville, Eugene as vice president of advanced planning and Bob as VP of switching sales. We decided early on to go big and go bold. Building on the success we had in inviting the giants of telecom to the launch of Digital World in Florida, we decided that this time we would also invite the titans of business and industry. The conference theme was Towards the Intelligent Universe, a moniker that eventually faded from memory. Since we seemed to own the 'World' category, we decided to declare OPEN World, for Open Protocol Enhanced Networks (engineers love acronyms). Once again, the good ship Northern would rally its crew by declaring a date, a place, and an announcement.

Somehow, that led us to chartering a ship. I can't remember how we came to the decision, but we decided to do the seminar on a cruise ship sailing out of Florida. Considering the Holland America line for the gig, we sent Bob and his wife, Ann, off to the closest cruise as secret shoppers (a hard job, but someone had to do it). Satisfied the cruise line met the standard required for our guests, we went to the company and, in a cruise-industry first, chartered the *SS Rotterdam* for two back-to-back trips from Miami to Freeport, Grand Bahama. The first cruise invited the top 500 global telecom industry leaders, and the second the Fortune 500.

Some thought we were crazy, but Walter and Derek loved the idea and supported our plan. Leaving the meeting with them after gaining their approval, Eugene, Bob, and I just looked at each other, somewhat surprised we had pulled it off. Bob said, "Ah, some people thought we were nuts. They might be right."

We were never relieved of our existing responsibilities, so the following year seemed like a blur. We were required to keep the event confidential from our competitors, so we worked on a need-to-know basis. Following the KISS principle—keep it simple, stupid or, in the case of Walter, keep it simple, sir!—we reported solely to Walter and Derek. I don't think we had a formal budget. Reaching primarily into the R&D organization for people and product, we had to innovate, create all the seminar content, organize everything from invitations to operational logistics, and do it twice. We decided that no cruise was complete without a black-tie gala, so we also booked Victor Borge to provide the entertainment on the first cruise and Tony Bennett the second.

One aspect of the event that concerned us early on was compiling the guest list. Fortunately, that was made easier by some changes at the top of the corporation. While Walter Light was an active and energetic champion of Northern's technology, he needed help both in consolidating the company's position in the United States and expanding beyond the boundaries of North America. In 1982, Walter became chairman and CEO, and Edmund B. Fitzgerald became president.

Many called him Fitz, but he was known affectionately in-house as Big Ed. Fitzgerald was extremely tall and had a commanding presence. An engineer, former Korean-war Marine commander, and a member of America's corporate elite, he was a consummate gentleman, team builder, and a good listener who embraced the corporate culture with ease. Also notable and endearing to Canadian employees was the connection to Gordon Lightfoot's iconic ballad *The Wreck of the Edmund Fitzgerald*. The Great Lakes freighter, owned by his shipbuilding family, had been named after Big Ed's father and plied the Lakes before a storm took her and all hands to the bottom of Lake Superior. (In Big Ed's office in a grand old southern mansion in Nashville, I saw the shipbuilder's huge model of the *Edmund B. Fitzgerald*, the largest ship on the Lakes, displayed in a beautiful glass case.)

Walter and Ed travelled the world together and had no problem contributing to the invitation list for the OPEN World conference. Walter covered the global services providers and Ed the Fortune 500. They knew all the customers and, more important, the customers knew them.

Never content with doing just enough, Bob, Eugene, and I ended up creating the equivalent of a trade-show exhibit with product demonstrations, concept models, working prototypes of a new line of digital business terminals with liquid crystal displays, and integrated voice and data products. The latter included Displayphone, an industry first, combining a telephone with a small computer terminal and keyboard for voice and data functionality in one unit.

Custom built for the ship, we designed the exhibit for the first-class passenger lounge after removing and storing the furniture. Unable to fit everything into the lounge, we also brought along Design Interpretive's mobile research lab, a 30-

foot Airstream trailer. We wanted to invite guests to personally contribute to the live research for the new terminals displayed in the exhibit. They might not have been typical users, but they were very big choosers with very deep pockets.

Seminars and presentations were scheduled throughout the two-night cruises, including my speech, entitled "Congeniality," scheduled to be delivered in the middle of the day, number five on a list of ten talks. As we rehearsed the presentations in Ottawa a month before the event, we discovered we couldn't fit everything on the day's agenda, so my talk was moved from the lounge to the theatre during the gala evening. The result—which I think was revenge by Eugene and Bob—was that I ended up as the opening act for Borge and Bennett. I needed to quickly re-write and reposition the talk as entertainment, renaming it "Human Touch (Batteries Not Included)." We produced a video to heighten the entertainment value and serve as my introduction on stage.

We boarded the *Rotterdam* in New York for transit to Miami, picking up the Airstream trailer, all the staging equipment, and Victor Borge's white custom-built grand piano. On the voyage south, we had to install the exhibit in the first-class lounge, set up the stage and lighting, build a custom production and projection booth for the theatre, and anchor the Airstream to the rear deck so guests could participate in real-time behavioral research.

One day before the first passengers arrived, the executive presenters boarded the ship for their dress rehearsals. Things didn't go well. During the dry run, we had a lot of birthing pain problems synchronizing lighting, sound, and a full-stage rear projection system that featured 16 images and 32 slide projectors. As the problems mounted, Walter became ever more frustrated and anxious about the event and the imminent arrival of guests. As he was wont to do, he lost his temper with Norbert Frischkorn, our onboard production manager, and shouted, "I want that guy fired. Get me someone who knows what they're doing." Walter promptly retreated to his upper deck cabin. Outraged, Norbert stormed to his cabin somewhere close to the water line and started to pack.

Walter's PR vice-president came to our rescue. He dispatched his staff with producer Richard St. John to get Norbert out of his cabin, while a few of us went with the VP up to Walter's cabin. After what seemed like a very long time, Walter answered the door. The VP calmly informed him that Norbert owned the production equipment, including the lights, projectors, and production consoles, and that without a personal apology the seminar would not and, indeed, could not go on. Walter knew doing the right thing was more important than any point of principle or pique. He joined us in the ship's theatre, apologized, shook hands, and, to everyone's delight, especially Norbert's, exchanged a hug.

Both cruises were a great success, with all our guests and staff having a wonderful time. The techie stuff was kept to an appropriate level in the presentations so that the same program could be delivered to everyone. The talks were thought provoking, even eye opening, for both business leaders and telecom executives. The focus throughout was business-to-business. We were demonstrating a real commitment to creating something that had real value for them.

Half the audience was made up of spouses, who were free to attend seminars or just enjoy the ship. Many on one cruise relaxed by the pool being charmed by Victor Borge as he strolled the deck flirting with every woman he met. On the other cruise, Tony Bennet never came out of his cabin. Many also stopped by the Airstream trailer and interacted with the prototypes, which provided us with a wonderful opportunity to see essentially non-business people using the technology. We loved having them there. The feedback was invaluable.

The spouses, of course, also attended the gala performances and so had the opportunity (or was it the burden) of experiencing my talk on stage in the ship's 500-

seat theatre. Thankfully, the talk was a big hit. By the time we finished the revisions and repositioning back in Ottawa, the presentation featured a video to the soundtrack of *The Music Man* and the song *Ya Got Trouble* ("Ya got trouble/Right here in River city!/With a capital "T"/And that rhymes with "P"/And that stands for Pool"). The video closed with a photo of me holding an unplugged orange extension cord. I then appeared on stage dressed in the same clothes and holding the same cord and delivered my talk. It's a good thing we didn't get carried away or the entire Broadway cast and orchestra would have entered playing *Seventy-six Trombones*.

All the presentations during the cruises were organized around "the five Cs:" continuity, compatibility, congeniality, cost-effectiveness, and control. As Mr. Congeniality, I opened my presentation with a photo of Leonardo's Vitruvian Man with a caption that read, "From Renaissance Man to today's Pac-Man, the human touch has played a key role in the advancement of technology." Other quotes appeared on screen as I emphasized user values and benefits: "A touch-tone telephone is so congenial that we live in fear of a toddler dialing Hawaii." "Congeniality of interface is the most challenging behavioral problem we have ever faced." I closed by repeating all five Cs and turned the stage over to the stars. Victor noted my spiel and, looking down at his keyboard, commented, "This should have been written in the key of seven Cs."

The event went off without a hitch to our customers' great delight and our competitors' dismay and frustration. We had no idea if it would work, never asked 'what if', and learned once again that there no limits when an organization has the passion and commitment to do whatever it takes to succeed.

Ed Fitzgerald summed up that commitment in his closing remarks on both cruises: "To turn our ideas into reality, we are making a public commitment to invest $1.2 billion in research and development for OPEN World over the next five years. By anybody's standard, that's a substantial wager. It reflects Northern Telecom's confidence in communications as the cornerstone of information management and in our own future." Truth be known, we invested a lot more than that. Armed with Ed's commitment, and then some, we set out to deliver on the promise.

Walter became the company chairman and Ed became CEO in 1984. Until Light's retirement in 1985, the dynamic duo expanded the corporate presence around the globe. Driven by product success and the corporation's longstanding commitment to be close to customers and their markets, massive expansion began to take place beyond North America within a rapidly changing industry. In the period between Digital World and OPEN World, ITT tried to develop a digital portfolio, failed, and withdrew from the telecommunications market altogether. The lesson learned, repeated from my lab book years before, still applied: "Without reach, there is no challenge. Without risk, there is no reward. Without vision, there is no future." The products and the promise were real. They had reach and risk and were presented in the context of a vision shared by every employee.

Ed Fitzgerald championed and embodied Northern's "product first" vision. He drew on all the resources of the corporation to excel and customers believed his promise. The bond was sealed by his personal integrity and ability to listen. During his term, Northern's revenue rose from $1.7 billion to more than $5 billion.

With the success of Digital World and OPEN World behind us, Northern and BNR also began to experience the natural repercussions of growth. Employee churn remained remarkably low, though some hairline cracks began to emerge. A couple of senior R&D executives left in personal frustration, only to return after discovering the grass wasn't greener on the other side of the fence after all.

Under a cloud of some controversy, colleagues Michael Cowpland and Terry Matthews left Microsystems International way back in 1972, forming Mitel to enter the small PBX market. They were accused of poaching friends and colleagues, including a few of mine. While litigation was discussed at one meeting I attended, the decision was made not to pursue any legal action. We concluded that we at BNR and Northern should expect to incubate lots of start-ups as a result of being very successful. That could only help Ottawa become a world-class centre of innovation and that was a winning scenario for everyone. We were right. Over the years, dozens of entrepreneurial businesses were created and thousands of new careers launched. Mitel was successful and later sold to British Telecom. Mike went on to found the graphics processing software firm Corel in 1985 and Terry founded Newbridge in 1986 to create data and voice networking products. Jozef Straus left the BNR labs in 1981 to found JDS Optics, which would become JDS Uniphase, a fiber-optic powerhouse. Throughout it all, our personal friendships endured.

As Northern grew, the result of product innovation and market success, the repercussions affected the executive management of Northern and BNR. Corporate governance was changed to reflect U.S. and international growth. In reaction to pressure from our competitors declaring that the U.S. subsidiary was not *really* an American company and, therefore, shouldn't be receiving American government contracts, the roles were split. Ed Fitzgerald, as an American with close ties to the Republican establishment during the Reagan years in Washington, moved his office to a colonial mansion in Nashville. Derek Davies would later join him, and Des Hudson, a Bell Canada executive who understood the telecom market, was named president of the American subsidiary, Northern Telecom Inc. (NTI)

Sometime during this period, I was promoted to assistant vice-president, Design Interpretive, the first AVP appointment in BNR (to my surprise, it came with a company car) and DI moved back onto the central campus and took over a metal-clad building, named the Sugar Shack, located behind new lab buildings. We once again placed our own stamp on the space, adding a courtyard to the north to give the designers north light (designers love north light) and creating an atrium front entrance. Northern got out of the satellite business in 1977, leaving it to SPAR Aerospace to further develop the Canadarm, and we claimed the former satellite group's research lab trailer, attaching it to the building water supply and building employee showers for campus joggers.

Inside, we were finally able to provide space for our prototype lab and created our best ever beanbag chair conference room. We marketed it as the ultimate client meeting space, given that we noticed no pinstripe could sit in a beanbag chair without loosening his collar and tie. I can't recall a customer ever refusing the seat. The beanbag room became part of BNR folklore and a destination point for customer visits.

BNR placed a high priority on customer engagement from the very beginning. Listening to customers was far more powerful than playing catch-up with competitors, and customers came to the labs in droves, from CEOs to heads of state. Nothing motivated the troops better than a parade of black limos pulling up to the front door of the Sugar Shack and groups of pinstripes touring the labs.

Customer visits were very big events. Northern sales executives, many of whom came out of the telcos, understood leverage and loved to use Ottawa to open and close their deals. So did every CEO I ever encountered. BNR remained the flagship destination for high-profile customers, particularly when it became time to close a deal with flagship customers negotiating contracts worth hundreds of millions, if not billions, of dollars. These meetings became so frequent and successful that BNR had to start billing expenses back to the host sales executives for things like airport transportation, limousines, catering, and dinners. The smart sales guys had found a way to avoid using their own budgets.

Walter Light loved bringing customers to BNR's main campus, partly to address our customers' greatest anxiety, namely security of long-term supply, and partly because I think he just loved being there. During one high-level customer visit, I was in the middle of a presentation when I noticed his seat was empty. There was only one door out of the room and it hadn't opened. Then I noticed that the heavy blackout curtains were moving in a very irregular manner. A short time later, he emerged from under the curtains and, ever the engineer, declared to everyone that the banging radiator was disrupting my presentation and he was trying to fix it. Unfortunately, the banging radiator continued.

Over time, Design Interpretive became a destination point of customer visits if for no other reason than every visit was memorable. Customers could see and feel whole products rather than components, lab tests, and prototype fabrications. DI evolved to the point that it became a stand-alone mini-conference centre.

Visiting BNR as part of closing one major deal, Ed Fitzgerald asked that, in addition to the general tour, the DI centre be the main meeting location and asked me to join the group for dinner later that evening and speak on behalf of BNR before his closing remarks. Following dinner in a private room of the Four Seasons Hotel in downtown Ottawa, my speaking requirement complete, Ed came forward for his closing remarks. Before he could say a word, the customer CEO rose to his feet, wine glass in hand, and said, "Ed, there's no need. It's a deal." Listening to the resounding applause, I knew I had just witnessed salesmanship at its understated best.

This was a great time to work for BNR and Northern. Recruiting drives brought new blood that re-invigorated our staff and it was common to hear, "I've got the best job in the world." I loved going to work every day and so did everybody else. Products and customers mattered and BNR was firmly entrenched in the corporate vision of Northern Telecom. As a product designer and designer of the BNR corporate identity, I could not have asked for more.

Back at the main labs, when Don Chisholm moved over to Northern as executive vice president for technology and innovation in the mid-seventies, Dennis Hall, a fine man considered a prime in the transition from analog to digital switching, took over as president of BNR from 1976 to 1981. Dennis invited me into a new and wonderful opportunity.

He recognized that using the technology of stored-program control could create a new market disruption, fundamentally changing the function of the telephone operator for the first time. Telephone operator jobs were still restricted to the same buildings as the central office switches, as they had been from the earliest days of the industry. The central offices were usually housed in the most expensive real estate in the cores of any city and, because of shift work and the personal security required for a workforce made up mostly of women, unions demanded that the employees be provided with late-shift taxi service. Operating costs were huge. But by using the power of stored-program control, which was the base of our digital revolution, operator jobs could be located remotely. Real-estate costs could be reduced drastically and operators could work closer to home.

The Telephone Operator Position System, or TOPS (damn engineers and their acronyms) emerged because design engineers discovered what they believed was an opportunity to attack our AT&T Goliath in the marketplace by further capitalizing on the digital revolution and the integration of voice and data. This was a major technological discontinuity. The product was so revolutionary that Bell Canada assigned a senior supervisor to our team and I ended up speaking to the annual Canadian conference of the Communications Workers of America.

Since the days of operators sitting in rows at switchboards, the technology had remained electromechanical. With this fundamental shift, it seemed the only remaining constant was the operator headset. We already knew the operators from extensive R&D leading up to the design of the Venture headset, which used the world's first electret noise-canceling miniature microphone and was later licensed under a royalty agreement to Sony.

Stretching our experience, we researched everything from workflow analysis to user needs assessment, and from graphic user interface to the ergonomics of workstations and chairs. By the time the TOPS workstation hit the market, we were commissioned to design a complete office for Bell Canada on top of a high-rise business development in Toronto, one in a shopping mall in Juneau, Alaska, and one in the tower of Cinderella's castle at Disney World in Florida (where operators taking a break simply walked out onto the turret). It would have been a great place for Rapunzel to let down her hair. AT&T was once again left flat-footed, one step behind and without a competitive vision. Even the world-renowned Bell Labs, which we always treated with great respect, lacked an alternative in the works.

The other new product that was particularly notable for DI and me involved a significant performance upgrade to the SL-1, still the world's most successful digital PBX. The product would be renamed Meridian to reflect the system's global ambitions, the transition from electromechanical to electronic terminals, and the many new performance values that included Meridian voicemail. As always with our event-driven company, Northern announced an international customer seminar for the new product, this one to be held in Laguna Beach, California, hosted by Des Hudson, the president of the American subsidiary, Northern Telecom Inc. (NTI).

With the date selected, Des invited Eugene Lotochinski and me to a dry run of the seminar in Dallas on the basis of our OPEN World experience. The dry run did not go well at all. Dismayed by the result, Des stopped the meeting, invited Eugene and me down front, and asked if we would please take full control. It meant a complete restart from the basics, but without any change in the date of the seminar.

Once again, I found myself up to my neck in event marketing and on an unforgiving schedule. Eugene and I threw ourselves into the task and created a production to showcase the new capabilities, complete with multiple laser beams and an actor playing Ferdinand Magellan, first circumnavigator of the world, to announce the Meridian product line. The seminar was a customer success and a competitor challenge. (We didn't tell management about the near disaster when a power cable caught fire.)

Des was very pleased and asked Eugene to invite me back to Nashville to join him for a thank-you dinner, with a promise to fly me home to Ottawa on the corporate jet. Exhausted, I gladly accepted the invitation. Arriving in Nashville, we went directly to the restaurant where I got much more than a meal. Des presented me with a custom-designed piece of Stueben Glass crystal—called "Creativity"—and, to my tremendous surprise, offered me the job of vice-president of marketing for Northern Telecom Inc. Even in my state of shock, I could sense an exciting new adventure ahead.

6 STAKING NEW GROUND

The timing of the offer was opportune. I had become so impressed with the performance of Design Interpretive and the quality of its staff that I was beginning to feel a sense of diminishing personal returns and a need for change. The group, numbering in the low 50s, was fully engaged in behavioral research and user-centric design. I had become tired of talking about design and always pushing. I decided to go to the other side and pull. On the other side, they didn't value design. It was largely invisible. The marketing job held out the promise of a fresh and challenging adventure.

Digital World had changed communications forever. BNR had achieved world-class status and was flourishing. Northern Telecom, along with BNR, had become a multinational corporation and employer of choice. The investment was in place to address the next market disruption and technology discontinuity brought about by lasers, fiber optics, and the resulting insatiable appetite for bandwidth on demand. BNR/Northern was leading the way in redesigning and building new communications capabilities, and the demand for ease, speed, and depth of access provided the impetus. There was no better time for me to rise to the next challenge in my pursuit of fulfillment and adventure.

It would be wrenching to leave BNR, but, thankfully, my Dutch bride, the lovely Yolanda whom I met while she worked at BNR and who was now the mother of our two small boys, loved the idea. I also had the approval of John Roth, my boss and president of BNR, though he was not enthusiastic. I have never forgotten the feeling that he was somehow disappointed. To this day, I wonder if I conveyed some sense of disloyalty to BNR, or to John, or my staff, or all three.

I recall using the phrase among the DI group that I was "joining the enemy." It was common for my colleagues in industrial design to refer to marketing as the enemy because all too often marketing destroyed the integrity of the design on a product's way to market: vinyl roofs on cars, phony wood grain on TVs, French-provincial coffin-shaped stereos, even leather-clad Contempras. Averse to reach and risk and, indeed, to innovation, marketing was content to replicate what their competitors offered. One colleague remarked after failing to get a new product past the marketing VP, "I knew I was dead in the water when, in frustration with his inability to express why he didn't like the product, he said, 'Why would I want it when my competitor doesn't have it?'"

I discovered in my earliest days of recruiting staff, that designers' portfolios were filled with product designs that represented what they liked and were often short of products that made it to market. The contrast and explanations they offered were amazing. They either discounted the responsibility for getting the product past the resistance of marketing, or they lacked the passion to pursue innovation in spite of the odds. Being from the school of hard knocks and with innovative product success behind me, I knew that innovation and marketing was mission critical. I agreed with business guru Peter Drucker that "Business has only two basic functions: Marketing and innovation. Marketing and innovation produce results. All the rest are costs." I had long since confirmed my feelings that innovation and marketing go together like a horse and carriage. In supra sync, they present the vision of the corporation to the world. I loved being involved with both.

Successful designers who joined the enemy were rare cats, but it appealed to my sense of challenge and adventure as well as my feelings of diminishing returns. As a champion of innovation, when the opportunity was presented I thought of Frodo in *The Fellowship of the Ring*, saying, "I will take the ring though I do not know the way." The thought probably occurred because at the time I had named my sailboat Elrond, after the Lord of Rivendell.

I began the adventure by seeking a work visa, commuting to Nashville, and selling our Ottawa home. With everything complete and a new home purchased, Des Hudson sent the corporate jet to Ottawa for our relocation. While we waited for our furnishings to arrive by truck, I booked the family into a small suite hotel frequented by country music stars and musicians on Nashville's famous Music Row, which, to my two young boys' delight, featured a guitar-shaped swimming pool. It was to be a wonderful period in our lives.

Des Hudson, a fine family man and people person, created a family atmosphere and a close fraternity. Consistent with our Northern culture and family commitment, at one company picnic following weeks of hilarious rehearsal, we executives performed Swan Lake dressed in pink tutus made by our wives. To end the show, our chief information officer (also wearing a tutu), drove onto the stage riding his Harley to the song *Leader of the Pack*. What might seem like common sense today wasn't then. Pinstripes were expected to be remote.

As Canadian resident aliens, our wives could not get work permits, resulting in lots of volunteer work to engage with the community. Community altruism just felt natural. They campaigned for, and created, a secure shelter for battered women while we road warriors were instructed to bring home all the the hotel provided toiletries we could get our hands on. When they opened the shelter, there were enough supplies to provide for the women and their children for a year.

The U.S. company was young and the location was new, so all the executives came from someplace else. I already knew many of the people who migrated with the expansion into the U.S. and they were supportive when required, though many didn't feel another marketing executive was necessary and wondered who was going to pay for it. Patience, perseverance, and a lot of good humour were required. Without Des Hudson's passion to create a powerhouse U.S. subsidiary, the job might not have turned out well. My boss was my champion.

Vice-president of U.S. marketing was a staff job with an expense budget and a total staff of eight, including executive assistants. The team included a director of marketing communications, two managers and an assistant to co-ordinate advertising and trade shows, an assistant vice-president of market development, and a director. Navigating through the corporate marketing ranks was challenging. The executive VP of marketing was a good guy, a classic telco-trained sales executive happy to nurture and otherwise stay out of the way.

Starting from scratch, I discovered something that would come up again and again throughout my career. People know what they are doing and are usually under-employed. Arriving in a new job, the first thing to do is to listen. Rather than pushing, best results emerge from pulling and empowerment.

Because Northern Telecom had evolved from a branch-plant manufacturing heritage, Bell Canada was virtually the only customer through the better part of a century. Who needs marketing? What marketing there was, meant selling licensed product and rewriting brochures. Before Contempra, Bell and Northern had never launched an original product into the market, being content with replicating designs from Western Electric and AT&T. Frankly, with the rare exception of people like Derek Davies, Northern never really understood the difference between marketing and sales in spite of sales reaching $30 billion. When I got involved with Digital World, Derek was the only one who understood marketing, brand equity, and market positioning.

Marketing, such as it was, was driven by an engineering value set rooted in the belief that every sale was a technical sale to technical people. The market might just as easily have been seen as a place to buy vegetables. Marketing and sales materials read like the back-page technical specifications in a car brochure. Advertising was 100 percent print based and almost exclusively in trade magazines. A few staff had experience outside Northern, but the vast majority had come up within the company, being promoted based on personal aptitude and career development opportunities. They were usually labeled marketing communications people, but were always connected to sales and always financed as a service expense.

Marketing executives, almost without exception, were engineers who had moved up the ranks because they knew the product and the customer and had shown skill in smooth talking their way to a sale. Thank goodness, they were very good at it. At any given time, driven by the expediency of the organization's development, they had titles featuring marketing, sales, or, when they couldn't decide, marketing/sales.

Business plans wrapped marketing, sales promotion, marketing communications, and advertising into a single pot that was used as a contingency reserve throughout the year. Needless to say, expense reduction ruled the day and long-range planning was quarter to quarter. The plans were managed at the divisional level merely as a sales plan in the operating budget. There was no consolidated view across the company.

At the corporate level, marketing communications and advertising were a battleground for control. Corporate public relations believed it held the purview of institutional advertising as part of its corporate relations mandate. The various divisions believed they owned the function. The reality was just two dogs fighting over the same biscuit. Any corporation that continues to fight over marketing as an expense versus an investment is destined to waste a lot of money, resources, and time. I've never experienced a return on expense other than simple cost reductions or cost avoidance, welcome as those might be. But a return on investment can impact decisions on new plants, equipment, and inventories. Investment faces out, expense faces in.

I experienced some culture shock. To me as an R&D guy, return on investment meant reach, risk, and vision. Innovation meant new product that resulted from the passion and commitment to get things done. Power and control simply meant being empowered to commit the dollars and resources. I wondered what I had done to my family and myself.

Believing it's better to listen before you talk and to walk before you run, I spent a lot of time checking out the lay of the land before making any waves. As part of the regular operations review process, Des Hudson brought his cabinet—including his CFO, CIO, and my boss, the executive VP of marketing—along in the corporate jet to meetings with the various divisions. I tagged along and just listened with great interest to the many conversations. Northern ran great operation reviews, but I noticed there were few, if any, strategic discussions. Strategy and tactics were usually clumped together without any time frame. They usually just merited two charts at the beginning of the annual operating plan. Few seemed to appreciate that strategy and tactics are not the same thing, that strategy is where you are going and tactics are how to get there.

I asked myself the question again and again, "Who in this room owns the strategy?" It was always the same answer. Des Hudson owned it and he also had the budget. Who was managing the strategy and budget on his behalf? No one. Seizing the opportunity, I defined my role to my liking and used his budget as my budget. I set the first strategic objective as changing marketing from an expense to an investment.

I discovered the market development function was pushing on a rope, telling the divisions what was wrong. The team was working in the classic staff role of "I'm from headquarters and I'm here to help." I challenged them to reach outside the company and bring about new strategic value through analyses of the industry, the competition, and the market.

Marketing communications was more difficult. With power and control decentralized and distributed and functioning as a committee, everyone's budget was below critical mass. To make matters worse, corporate relations controlled brand management out of Canada, which was primarily focused on corporate identity. Corporate relations held an annual review while looking through a rear-view mirror. Following extensive discussion with divisional executives, I launched a full analysis of all work in progress.

My concerns with marketing communications were trivial when compared to our relationship with our advertising agency, J. Walter Thompson (JWT), one of the world's largest agencies. The Northern account wasn't even centralized, resulting in individual accounts in Canada, the U.S., and the U.K. Any chance of investment leverage was lost in interdependent subcommittees in both companies. In truth, JWT, also left pushing on a rope, treated the account as a bread-and-butter retainer, using it as a training ground for creative and account staff. I discovered that the only thing worse than underemployed staff, is underemployed agency resources. Everyone loses.

After assuming control of Northern's U.S. account, one of my first acts was to visit JWT's headquarters in Chicago's Sears Tower. I was determined to rattle the relationship, so I informed the account managers that I was considering placing the account under review. In industry jargon, that meant we were unsatisfied and were opening the account to competitive bids. In industry practice, it was second only to being fired. It meant the agency had to fight to keep the account. Having gained their attention, I also told them that I believed 51 percent of the problem lay with us, the client, and that future success depended on creating a new relationship.

I introduced JWT to our new code of business ethics, which meant entertainment expenses were to be paid directly by Northern, inverting the conventional practice of ad agencies having big-ticket client expense accounts. I challenged them to consolidate all the work under way, and bring forward for review, in stages, a fresh advertising strategy that included creative alternatives and a two-year media plan. I insisted that I have unrestricted access to their creative executives, and they to me.

It was hard work and met with some resistance along the way, but it was also a lot of fun for everyone. They already knew Northern was a bread-and-butter account and a lousy client to work with. To them, I was a breath of fresh air, albeit cocky. The agency felt they at last had a client who understood their business and our staff felt someone was finally listening to them.

All the work and meetings concluded in a full-cabinet plan review and a presentation to both the American and corporate headquarters—a company first. The result was a fully authorized two-year media plan, along with a short tutorial on media buying as a cost-effective investment. The authorized plan allowed JWT's Canadian and U.K. work forces to be consolidated under the direction of the Chicago office, Northern's U.S. programs and budgets to be centralized, and, without reorganization, management and staff to remain close to their respective divisions and product management. This all happened because of the mindset change. We were making an investment, not managing an expense.

Experienced in corporate identity and market branding from creating the BNR program, I set out to introduce the company to market positioning, still a relatively recent concept at the time. Market positioning is strategic to marketing and advertising, as it sets a category of the mind that is timely and, more importantly, within the perceptions and values of target audiences. Northern needed something in addition to product-by-product differentials. The need was to create, build, and sustain a position to market that differentiated us from our competitors and their products. Doing it within customer perceptions would provide the umbrella for our new products.

After Digital World, we as an industry had talked and talked about the convergence of voice and data. Voice and data had become established categories of the mind with our targeted customers, who categorized suppliers accordingly. In America, AT&T owned telephony and IBM owned data processing. An issue of Business Week even featured an "AT&T versus IBM" cover.

A review of their positions to market showed they were both trying to shift from the category of the mind that each owned, to also covering the changing market. By doing so, they were confusing their customers as they tried to plan their future networks.

AT&T was all over the positioning map. The company's ads claimed, "From equipment to networking, from computers to communications…AT&T is the right choice." Their problem was that they were simultaneously trying to extend the category and carry old baggage. IBM, on the other hand, was trying to extend its category by making telephony products look and sound like data products. Having purchased Rolm, a rugged technology competitor for some Northern Telecom products, IBM ads said, "Introducing the IBM 9750 Business Communications System. Any connection between voice and data is purely intentional."

We didn't own either category, so our choice seemed to be to pick one or play both, which just left us in a reactive position. Our share of mind was in specific products rather than market position. But I thought we had an opportunity to take advantage of the confusion and create a new category that was timely and had staying power within the perception of our target audiences. We had the freedom of choice. By matching our position to market to a new category, we had the opportunity to be first in mind and first in category, redefining the boundaries of competition to provide the advantages of a leadership position. Rather than position our product initiatives to our competitors' products or category, the opportunity was to build upon our proactive position to market.

Enter *networking*. Being first didn't require us to be the largest but did require us to be proactive. Northern had shown time and again that it was adaptive in anticipating market discontinuity. We were reinforcing the promise of our Digital World and OPEN World commitment. We had products in the pipeline to prove it: broadband ISDN, data gateway, digital Centrex, network management, local- and wide-area networks, and new fiber products for network transmission. Together, market positioning and superior product were an unbeatable combination.

The market positioning idea of networking that I initially presented as a confidential white paper to Des Hudson suddenly became a key message and I found myself on the agenda for the annual sales conference only a month away. I asked Des if he wanted the presentation in the context of a dialog, and he replied, "I want it announced as our new position to market." As the draft speech circulated for comment, I was often asked, "But what does networking mean?" Detecting a product bias, I had to clarify the position: Networking is not a product position. It is a market position and category. As a category of the mind, its definition is as broad as all the layers of approval processes of all our customers. To define it is to narrow it.

It is a rare market event when a corporation has the opportunity to discover a new category emerging from the convergence of old and maturing businesses. Even more significant is the opportunity to make the position to market and the category of the mind one and the same. Position to market is a cumulative build brought about by presence, product, and continued market credibility, namely great success at the cash register.

With the position to market declared as a global initiative at the annual U.S. sales conference and publicly endorsed by Des Hudson, I hoped that I could simply get on with the job, but that was not to be. The conference audience didn't include product managers from the product divisions. It didn't include corporate executives from the head office in Canada. While I had successfully sold the two-year media plan that consolidated advertising, I hadn't appreciated that, in the euphoria of getting the position to market done, I had run afoul of the traditions of the corporate hierarchy that required seeking consensus or approval in advance. I had stepped on a lot of very sensitive toes, which meant weeks of getting on and off planes, having endless face-to-face meetings, and eating lots of humble pie. It wasn't that the hierarchical pinstripes disagreed with the market positioning; they just resented being ignored. The experience provided me with some great executive coaching and management training.

With both the market position resolved, and a two-year media plan in place, we launched an aggressive campaign that included a seminar for our newly opened Northern Telecom Institute for Information Studies, in co-operation with the Aspen Institute, at Wye Plantation in Maryland. We invited industry leaders and academics to lead two-and-a-half-day seminars designed for our customers' senior planners and strategists.

We launched Northern into a new world that included an industry first: the million-dollar purchase of the entire Fortune Magazine annual Fortune 500 edition (20 full-page colour ads). In addition to a global advertising campaign, we introduced radio through PBS, television through C-Span, and corporate events through sponsoring the PGA Tucson Open golf tournament.

True to my designer obsession, I demanded visual and copy continuity across all media, resulting in every ad being on a full-page white background. All copy was minimal and ended with the Northern Telecom logo as the punctuation mark. The bottom of every ad simply featured the word 'Networking' in bold upper case capital letters. My objective was profound simplicity!

According to agency insight, reader loyalty to advertising is always in the order of employees first, then competitors and customers who are looking for reassurance directly proportional to the size of their purchase. With the launch of the campaign in Fortune Magazine, thousands of copies were handed out at every office and plant throughout North America as employees entered the office. Due to printing schedules, the rest of the world received the edition a few days later.

The most successful ad, and my favourite, called "Children of The World" featured four naked babies surrounding an illuminated world globe on the floor. The copy read: "Understanding. Our children will be a lot better at it. In Northern Telecom's Intelligent Universe, sharing information, anywhere, anytime and in any form will be as easy as using the phone today."

Producing the ad was easier than getting its approval. Naked babies? Fretters emerged from everywhere and I was pressured to drop the ad. Fortunately, I had an answer. The agency, recognizing such possible sensitivity, had retained a top photographer (and a mother), allowed the babies' mothers on set, restricted the shoot to women only, and found four beautiful babies, including a Caucasian, African-American, Asian, and Hispanic. The photographer later told me she hadn't had as much fun on the set in years what with mothers chasing the laughing and running babies everywhere. Luckily, it wasn't a shoot with the director calling, "Quiet on the set!" To my great satisfaction, it was the most requested ad ever produced by Northern Telecom.

The Intelligent Universe, the OPEN World seminar, and the funded multi-year program were huge successes as verified by market research. By the time I left for my next adventure, yearly revenue, driven by product success and customer engagement, exceeded $5 billion and the marketing investment surpassed $50 million a year.

Success requires an unrelenting focus on product, vision, and the market. Success takes commitment, time, and discipline in investing in innovation, not thinking in terms of expense and service. Managing to the metrics of expense and service is the best way to constrain innovation, creativity, and corporate momentum. Being proactive versus reactive makes a big difference, and we were looking forward while our competitors were consumed in reaction. Being out in front of the market matters. Just ask a competitor what it costs to react or play product catch-up.

Fortunately, we had the vision, the product, and the market position. In spite of the many difficulties our massive international expansion entailed, our passion and commitment prevailed.

7 CHANGING THE OPTICS

Always forward looking, Northern's R&D investment in fiber-optic networks was central to the next great market discontinuity. The world's century-old, copper-based narrowband networks were going to be replaced by broadband networks with signals streaming along optical fibers and we were determined to be the first company to offer the switching and transmission products necessary to build and operate end-to-end fiber-optic networks. The product line to be launched in '90/'91, internally code-named FiberWorld, offered virtually limitless potential for services beyond voice and data to include text, images, and full-motion video.

In anticipation of the launch of this next great initiative, I was invited in late 1988 to join the transmission group in Atlanta as vice-president of market development. The FiberWorld products had been under development for several years and would require more years of investment before being phased into the world's networks. But, just as with Digital World, we were at least a year, if not more, ahead of our rivals in readying the new technology for the market and planned to announce our fiber vision to the world by the end of 1989. FiberWorld was a huge undertaking that required every piece designed from scratch with state-of-the-art technology.

Through the fall of the year, I commuted every week while my Nashville house went up for sale and new digs were sought out in Atlanta. For the sake of the kids, we moved the day before Christmas Eve so they could start at their new school on the first day of the new year. Their biggest concern was, "But how will Santa find us? How will he know where we live?" We reassured them and supported the message by making sure that the last thing loaded into the moving van and the first thing out was the carefully wrapped fully decorated Christmas tree, lights and all. Our first act in our new home was plugging in the tree. (We of course kept from them that wrapped presents were in boxes in the truck, coded with three small Xs, for three kids and three kisses.)

My boss in Atlanta was John Taylor, the transmission group VP and a good friend. He was a brilliant Scot with a PhD in physics, fiercely loyal to his staff, highly opinionated, determined, and cheap. He bought used furniture for his office and the staff always joked that he used each tea bag twice. Arriving for my first day on the job, John escorted me to an office at the end of a hall beside a noisy hydraulic freight-elevator shaft. I asked him what he expected of my job and whether there was any symbolism associated with the office location. He replied, "Figure it out. And given the opulence of the corporate headquarters you came from, I figured you needed to come down to earth." Gee, thanks.

Once again, as in my previous job, I had a title, no staff other than an executive assistant, and no budget. And, once again, just as in my previous job, I discovered that marketing and sales were managed as an expense and that long-range planning was defined as the next quarter's operating plan review. I again spent a couple of months discovering the lay of the land, meeting customers, and doing a job analysis of my peers and their accountabilities, including Taylor's, who was accountable for introducing FiberWorld and owned the budget for doing so.

Armed with my analysis, I presented my opinion of the job to John, laid out my initial strategy, and announced that because market development was an investment, his group budget was my budget. Following an animated discussion, he said, in typical Taylor fashion, "What took you so long?" Later that afternoon, he unceremoniously walked into my office by the elevator shaft, invited me to an empty office closer to his (that included a private balcony where I could smoke), and said, "Get some new furniture. You designers are all the same."

In many ways, my time in Atlanta felt like being at home. With the BNR regional lab next door, I was working with product guys, all purple people, and their spirit of innovation, dedication, and excellence. Having the BNR labs within walking distance of the headquarters for marketing and product-line management seemed like a gift from heaven. Researchers there were working closely with senior management in Ottawa—BNR president George Smyth, systems engineering VP Irving Ebert, and transmission VP Robert Pfeffer—who were leading the exploratory research and product development. We were also working with the lab in Harlow in the U.K. that was part of Standard Telephone and Cables Company (STC), formerly a unit of ITT. Ed Fitzgerald had bought ITT's stock in 1987 (27 percent of the company), a shrewd strategic move since the lab was the birthplace of optical fiber communications. Researchers there had pioneered the use of glass fiber to carry information in the 1960s. Another Harlow scientist in the 1930s had invented pulse code modulation, the basis for digital communications.

The transmission guys welcomed me with ease, which was quite a contrast to the often-complex process of navigating through the bureaucracy in corporate headquarters. They had passion, had secure R&D investment, and were driven by a schedule commitment. I felt privileged to work with them, although on occasion they could drive me nuts. They were classic engineers, analytical and pragmatic.

While focused on the intimate details of components within their own discipline, they had great trouble understanding the whole product experience and its value.

While attending an R&D review meeting back in Ottawa and seeing some early prototype product, I commented negatively on the state of the industrial design. Someone asked, "What's wrong with it? Nobody sees it anyway."

Restraining myself, I said, "They'll see it when we feature it at the product launch. They'll see it in trade shows and in the customer conference centre we're going to build in Atlanta."

Not getting it, he asked, "Can you be more specific?"

Avoiding expletives, I said, "It's not about good or bad or right or wrong. In this case, it just *sucks!*"

Shortly after, my former Design Interpretive group was fully engaged. I had kept in touch, of course, throughout my tenure in the U.S., calling on DI for help in marketing communications, exhibit design concepts, demo centers, and product branding while also working as their advocate and agent with the product divisions. But the folks in DI had failed to tell me how much resistance they were experiencing from the engineering side of things. Many meetings later, the result was a reenergized DI and a much better spirit of collaboration to help power a team that was already operating with a sense of destiny and purpose.

I soon discovered that the main source of anxiety in Atlanta was the need to retain sales and gain market share with the current product portfolio while they were in the process of making that portfolio obsolete. Impressed by their passion, determination, and commitment to pull it off, all I could do initially was help them with current product positioning for the transition. But the engineering mindset I'd battled in Nashville, where every sale was considered a technical sale to technical people, was alive and well in Atlanta.

I went to a local Porsche dealer and brought back a brochure of the new 911 Turbo. I showed the engineers the back cover, which had the car's performance specification contained in a black-bordered box. I suggested that it was there solely for performance junkies and gear-heads. The other 12 full-colour pages sold the emotive value to the purchaser. I helped them discover that the current portfolio wasn't about transmission performance specs. It was about selling customers an emotive value proposition of the whole product line through a commitment to forward compatibility, allowing customers to build out their current networks in anticipation of being first to market with more advanced technology. In other words, we were saying to our customers, "As an early adopter, buy now in anticipation of an increasingly competitive carrier market." It worked to the extent that some customers moved away from a wait-and-see attitude. I also coached the product management to embrace and push the corporate networking theme embodied in our position to market.

The new transmission equipment embodied the Optical Carrier (OC) standards that had evolved for transmission speeds in public fiber-optic networks. All our products had engineering-driven product names such as OC-128, OC-64, or OC-32, depending on the speed of the signals transmission. I didn't think those names were all that helpful in developing the market, so I found myself in the naming game yet again.

We decided that we would name the products by their function rather than by their performance value. The result was AccessNode instead of OC-64 for delivering signals over the local loop, and TransportNode instead of OC-128 for handling long-distance signals. It was a struggle to come up with an appropriate name for the juggernaut DMS switching platform that was the key bridge between broadband and narrowband networks. I sent a need-your-help note off to Roy Merrills, now president of NTI. A few days later he asked if I had considered SuperNode. Eureka. He nailed it. SuperNode it was.

Unfortunately, it also exposed a problem that would re-emerge later. The transmission group was abandoning the DMS prefix it had used for its product since the launch of Digital World many years before. There was a long-standing animosity between switching and transmission, exaggerated by the fact they had competing sales forces addressing the same customers, all chasing sales commissions and other compensation. While they attended the same annual sales conferences, they broke out into private meetings to hear their new sales plans and annual objectives. I attended the 1990 conference and, for the first time, a rep from transmission was named Salesman of the Year, which didn't bode well for the relationship between switching and transmission. This was about pride and money. When it came to product naming, the switching juggernaut was king of the roost and the gang there resented some clucking hen from transmission taking the lead. Following numerous discussions, a compromise was reached. To maintain continuity, the FiberWorld products would add the prefix DMS, creating DMS TransportNode, DMS AccessNode, and DMS SuperNode.

The whole FiberWorld development process was complicated by the fact that in March 1989, just a few months after my relocation to Atlanta, a new CEO had come on the scene. Intensifying global competition and the massive costs involved in Northern's expansion and investment in new technologies had badly affected the company's financial performance. Ed Fitzgerald reached outside the corporation for a hard-nosed, cost-cutting successor in the mold of John Lobb.

Paul Stern would be a challenge to both the culture and vision of Northern Telecom. He had a doctorate in solid-state physics from Britain's University of Manchester and, tellingly, loved being introduced as Dr. Stern. He had previously been an executive at several companies, including IBM, Unisys, and Rockwell. I later learned he had an affinity for product design, probably bolstered by his experience as CEO of Braun AG, Gillette's German subsidiary. Braun was famous for its products designed by equally famous industrial designer Dieter Rams, with whom Stern developed a personal friendship.

I first met him briefly when he came to Atlanta and gave a lengthy speech to the executives and management. I was just one amongst the crowd, but my first impression was that of a polished pinstripe determined to convey that there was a new boss in town. He understood power and control, and his meetings were often described inside as Stern "holding court." He had little interest in technology, focusing solely on expenses and other cost reductions, financial performance, and global sales expansion. Unfortunately, he considered R&D an expense rather than an investment and, during his years in office, reduced R&D spending substantially from almost 15 percent of revenues to 11 percent.

Stern was determined to shake up Northern's management and brought with him two former IBM executives, James Long, who became president of world trade, and Edward Lucente, who became executive vice-president of marketing. Lucente had a reputation for a slash-and-burn approach to management and had acquired the nickname 'Neutron Eddie', in honour of the neutron bomb, because after Ed visited a company, the buildings were still there but all the people were gone. The troika of Stern, Lucente, and Long took tight control of everything, pulling finance and human resources along with them. (Stern and Lucente were later paired in an internal song parody—*Dr. Doom and Neutron Eddie*—written and performed by DI's Chris White, thankfully produced before the YouTube era.)

Stern's cost-cutting ways had an impact across the corporation. He was on everyone's ass to cut back, including John Taylor's, while Neutron Eddie was busy attacking everyone's group marketing and sales programs. He was on a drive to restructure the corporation and within nine months had shuffled management, cut 2,500 jobs, and closed four plants. He took tough measures but did produce results. Expenses in 1989 fell 18.5 percent from the year before and profits went up 18 percent on a 13 percent increase in sales.

Having been raised in Mexico City and being fluent in Spanish, he soon increased sales by becoming the largest supplier to Mexico's leading cellular provider and later completed the purchase of Britain's STC, making Northern a significant player in both countries just as their telecom markets were deregulated and privatized. But his demanding, some say arrogant, ways drove quite a few executives out of the company and into the arms of competitors.

Though it had nothing to do with Stern, it was during this period that I began to question relevance and fulfillment in my work. I had transferred my values to marketing because I could see tangible results, but I was first, foremost, and always a product guy, heart and soul. Marketing or industrial design, it was always about design and about the simple proven creative process of problem-solution-benefit. Since the days of Don Chisholm, I had given myself permission to be my own patron. The only difference in the change from design to marketing was that in design I pushed and in marketing I pulled. In the process, I influenced new product innovation, brand equity, and corporate vision and market position. The work was fulfilling in the sense of taking on a challenge and winning, but the question I faced was, "What's next?" I was concerned that I risked being typecast as a staff troubleshooter, with a resulting feeling of being taken for granted. With a family whose children were reaching the age where stability mattered to their development, I began to think about a change. I loved being an industrial designer and innovator and working in R&D. That was what I loved to do. That had real relevance to my personal values.

I received a call early one morning in my Atlanta office from the managing director of design for Philips in the

Netherlands. He said he was soon retiring and asked if I was interested in being interviewed for his position. After an extensive discussion, I said yes. The next weekend I flew to Las Vegas to meet him for dinner and take a tour of a private suite exhibit used for restricted distributor disclosures at the Consumer Electronics Show. After a second interview with a top executive recruiting agency in New York, my Dutch wife and I were quietly invited to Phillips' global headquarters in Eindhoven for a final round of interviews. No one at Northern knew anything about it. I made a point of travelling on my own time, taking days off, and paying for any travel expenses, with the exception of Phillips paying for our travel to the Netherlands.

In what now seems like the most bizarre of days. I was picked up at the hotel and personally interviewed by every member of the board of management, starting with the president and CEO, which included executive assistants bringing in coffee on silver trays featuring Philips' custom china at every meeting (the Dutch always start a meeting with coffee). The day ended with a medical exam conducted by the managing director of health services who, thank goodness, was also a doctor. Meanwhile, Yolanda was picked up by the director of real estate and taken on a tour of executive-owned homes available for lease while the executives were on international postings. Then, hosted by the wife of the managing director of human resources, she was taken to lunch at a private club with a group of managing directors' spouses (I got a whack for suggesting they wanted to check out her table manners). That evening, we joined the head of human resources and his wife for dinner at an exclusive private country club frequented by members of the Philips family.

The whirlwind day complete, we headed back to Atlanta with assurances that all had gone well and that the board of management insisted that a North American must fill the position. Two weeks later, I was informed that because of the economic climate and declining revenues, the company decided to fill the position internally with the promotion of their design director from Italy. I didn't even get a consolation prize of an electric shaver.

Feet back on the ground, Yolanda and I agreed there was something to be learned from the experience. First, the choice for my next location would be based on the children's priorities and, second, that living again in an exclusive gated community was too isolated. We wanted the children to attend schools that had greater socioeconomic and cultural diversity. In a way, I was disappointed in not winning the position. But, then, when one door closes....

Paul Stern spent much of his first year in office on a leadership campaign, making the rounds of facilities to shore up his claim to the presidential throne. Following an operations review in Atlanta, I attended an executive dinner and came across Stern at the pre-dinner bar. Since this was our first, albeit casual, conversation beyond a nod and a handshake, I introduced myself. He replied, "I know who you are." My first thought was, how does he know me? Given his reputation to date, should I be worried?

He said he had met with my former design group in Ottawa and had a big idea for them. He did not go into any detail about what his big idea was. It struck me that he was in an almost playful, jousting mood. He asked what I thought and, jousting in return, my flippant, smart-assed, reply was, "It's probably not big enough," meaning that if he was serious there was only one guy—me—who could pull off any big design idea. Before getting sidetracked to another discussion, he said, "Call me." The conversation was very brief. As it turned out, it might have been the shortest executive job interview in corporate history. Other than briefly discussing the meeting with Yolanda, John Taylor, and BNR president George Smyth, I didn't think all that much more about it as I returned to my work on the FiberWorld launch.

FiberWorld was clearly a big idea with profound implications. It required a formal announcement at an event similar to the Digital World and OPEN World extravaganzas, but the world had changed. It was no longer acceptable for customers, especially governments, to accept lavish invitations at a supplier's expense. Forced to get a little creative, I decided that if our target audience couldn't come to us, we'd go to them. The result was a mobile conference centre that could be installed in a hotel ballroom. Completely self-contained, it featured a reception area, small private offices for guest calls, a custom oval table that sat 30, five rear-view projection screens, and integrated lighting and sound systems. Customers later praised its feeling of intimacy and privacy. Completely modular, we would use various components for the formal announcement in New York City and at other events around the U.S.

Plugging away on the FiberWorld market development, I got a call from David Vice, who had been Northern's president in the last half of the eighties when Ed Fitzgerald became chairman and CEO. Dave was a long-time champion of the transmission group and was now the corporation's vice chairman. He told me he was concerned that Northern was still primarily seen globally as a North American switch manufacturer and nothing more, and that the perception had to change. He said it was time to go big or stay home. We had already established a presence in Europe and Asia but had to make a much bigger splash on the global scene. The perfect venue, he said, was Telecom '91, the upcoming edition of the trade show and conference held every four years in Geneva, Switzerland, under the auspices of the International Telecommunications Union (ITU), an agency of the United Nations. Called the Olympics of telecommunications, it usually attracted more than a hundred thousand delegates, including corporate CEOs, government ministers, and heads of state. Dave asked, "Where better to state our vision and show our FiberWorld product?" Less a question than a decision and directive, I suddenly found myself up to my neck in new issues.

I still reported to John Taylor in Atlanta, but Vice insisted that I have an office in Mississauga, near Toronto, and report to him. Ed Lucente, Stern's executive vice-president of marketing who had set up an office in Tyson's Corner, Virginia, insisted that he owned anything associated with the name Tyson, including the T '91 initiative, and that I should report to him. I now had three bosses in two countries and an event to pull off on another continent. Things got complicated. At one point, the corporate controller's office called to say that I was in violation of corporate policy because I couldn't have two budgets in two different subsidiaries in two different countries at the same time. I asked him not to blame the victim but to find a solution. He did, assigning Terry Bartlett to be my personal controller for Telecom '91. It was a good thing, too, because Terry insisted on buying a hedge for millions of dollars in Swiss francs for the event still two years away. His prescience was critical in my meeting the budget during a period of significant currency fluctuations.

My three-bosses situation was never resolved. I took the office in Mississauga, refused an executive assistant, accepted a pass for executive underground parking, and got on with the task. All the T '91 staff, eventually numbering hundreds, were temporarily assigned from North America and Europe for the duration of the project, with the exception of Terry Bartlett, Ray Langton in Nashville, and Arno Schmidt, an assistant vice-president from Northern Telecom Canada. True to our corporate spirit, the level of co-operation and commitment was nothing short of motivational. That took the edge off the fact that I had two overlapping events with completely separate logistics. Telecom '91 was a huge undertaking, but at least the FiberWorld event, because of its much earlier scheduled start in October 1989, was under control and on schedule, allowing me to jump from one project to the other as required.

When I took on the responsibility for T '91, there was already a plan in place for our display, the project being under the control of Des Hudson, now president of Northern Telecom Europe. But because the event would come so hard on the heels of the launch of FiberWorld, I wanted to build the theme around the networking position to market we had already established. I stopped in for a visit with Des in London and, with his support, re-vectored the program to the expanded vision and prepared to run the gauntlet of corporate approvals. Feeling more like an executive producer than a VP of market development, I met with our exhibit designer in Basingstoke, U.K. before visiting the Geneva Exhibition and Convention Centre, Palexpo, to check out the site. The next couple of years were exhausting. I confirmed my status as an international road warrior, continuously traveling between Atlanta, Nashville, Dallas, Toronto, Ottawa, London, and Geneva. It was just my luck that Eastern Airlines went bankrupt during that time, taking my 500,000 air miles with it.

With Telecom '91 planning well in hand, I jumped back into FiberWorld and market development. The long lead-time projects, including the conference and demo centre in Atlanta, the mobile conference centre, the exhibit, and the operations and logistics for each event were all on schedule. The content was another matter. While the engineering folks focused on the product deliverables for the demo centre and trade shows, I concentrated on the material required for the product launch. Starting from scratch, we had to create everything from marketing collateral to all the seminar content, a special issue of *Telesis* magazine, product brochures, press releases, and executive speeches. The production lead times created a lot of pressure, but I was blessed with a lot of great people and reached out to a friend in Nashville, Ray Langton, a Brit and first-class operations guy, for additional operations management support. Ray was a great help.

I was spending most of my time in Ottawa, relying on the insights of George Smyth, Irving Ebert, and Robert Pfeffer. The event was approaching fast and getting everything right mattered. Close to the eleventh hour, the four of us met in George's office in Ottawa, all the while in constant contact with the purple teams in Atlanta, Harlow, Montreal, and Raleigh. We decided to reposition the product line, resulting in a name change, a tough decision with so much design and writing work underway, but the right thing to do. George, Irving, Rob, and I felt like managing editors running on passion and adrenalin. It was a lot of fun.

SONET—Synchronous Optical Network—had become the North American standard that allowed the interworking of transmission products from multiple vendors. Adding the SONET prefix, we positioned the portfolio as a multi-service ethernet platform. Going one step further, we named it S/DMS and stepped on a land mine. After just getting the switching division to accommodate the name SuperNode, they now needed to accept S/DMS SuperNode. Much discussion and soothing of egos ensued.

Forced to have production printing done locally in Ottawa, we worked many late nights with the *Telesis* editor and Design Interpretive's graphic designers. Down to the wire and with no flight available from Ottawa, John Taylor sent the corporate jet to Ottawa to pick up the printed material and me, suggesting that the material, with the ink still wet, get the seats while I should travel as baggage. I went directly to his office and personally delivered the material. Leaving my office later that evening, I went to the dark parking lot only to remember that I'd left my car four days earlier at Atlanta's main airport terminal, not anticipating that my return fight would be to a private terminal miles away. Too tired to get it, I took a taxi home.

Thanks only to the passion and conviction of everyone involved, the launch a few days later in New York City was a great success. We positioned the New York event primarily to the trade press and Wall Street, taking an indirect shot across the bows of our competitors. It was intended to demonstrate our commitment to the next technical discontinuity and market disruption in telecommunications. It was followed quickly by the FiberWorld Planners Conference in West Palm Beach, Florida, a customer-only event featuring in-depth seminars, the official opening of the demo centre in Atlanta, and a completely new exhibit at SuperComm in Dallas featuring FiberWorld products over an underlying graphic theme of Children of the World. All were great successes. Once again, the spirit of collaboration and our product innovation carried the day.

A couple of months later, I received a heads-up call from George Smyth informing me that Paul Stern was going to announce a corporate design centre of excellence, and that I was to be the vice-president in charge. I don't recall if George ever asked me if I wanted the job or had even been asked to check it out. To this day, I have no idea who Stern talked to before making his decision. But I was intrigued.

I said yes to the job (and to the relocation to wherever that might be since nobody had mentioned it). George assumed it was a cabinet position in Ottawa. Des Hudson, operating out of the United Kingdom as president of Northern Telecom Europe, wanted the position to be located in London so I could get a feel for the nature of the European market and be close to the BNR labs in Harlow. I was excited about the prospect of London. Given that I had a Dutch wife with lots of family in Europe and three young children, I saw it as the opportunity of a lifetime. Soon after, I was pulled out of a meeting by my executive assistant in Atlanta and informed that a very irritated chairman was on the phone. Paul Stern's first words were, "Tyson, the goddamn job is in Ottawa. Do you want it or not?" Unable to resist, I asked, "Does that mean I can no longer negotiate?"

Yolanda, who was so supportive of the move to Phillips, saw this as the same job within Northern Telecom and was delighted at the prospect of returning to our hometown, as were the kids. Within minutes of Paul's call to me, George called to welcome me back and told me that my original phone number was still available. Not too long after, to the children's delight, I booked the longest stretch limo I could find for the trip to the airport and, after seven years in the United States, returned with my family to Ottawa.

But before we did, I experienced one of life's great moments. My son, Kevin, asked me to talk to his Grade 2 class about advertising on career day. I went to his classroom only to discover that the speaker before me was a U.S. Air Force Top Gun pilot dressed in full combat gear, complete with helmet and fold-down visor. After his inspiring talk, I wondered how I could compete. I remembered a little trick I taught my kids. Using a black felt marker, pad and easel, I invited one of the children to draw one line of any shape on the pad, which I then converted to a cartoon of a jet fighter in flight. I asked another child to draw another line and quickly created a cartoon of Bart Simpson. With Bart's help, I tossed my notes and talked about what they already knew about advertising, from Sesame Street to McDonalds' golden arches. As British playwright James M. Barrie said, "Life is a long lesson in humility."

I was now VP of corporate design for Northern Telecom, located at BNR's Ottawa headquarters, still VP of market development for the transmission group in Atlanta, and corporate VP for Telecom '91 reporting to offices in both Ontario and Virginia. I now had four bosses in two divisions in two subsidiaries in two countries, three business cards, one hat, and yet, sadly, only one paycheque. My relocation back to Canada added to the complexity. Classified in the U.S. as a resident alien with a green card, I was one year short of vesting in old age security retirement benefits. To ensure my future qualification, Northern, to its credit, created a U.S. subsidiary registered in Delaware where I was one of the very few employees. The net result was a paycheque in U.S. dollars for the next year while I was officially granted the legal status of "non-resident, resident alien," with a postal address in San Francisco, the office of our immigration lawyers.

With my family stabilized in our new home, I got back to the tasks immediately at hand, specifically the planning for Telecom '91 in Geneva. Ian Craig, a friend and colleague from the earliest days of BNR, had established a beachhead for Northern at Telecom '87, but to meet our more ambitious goals, we were aiming for at least twice the scale and more than twice the budget. In 1987, the hot topics were the convergence of computers and communications, and the wonders of ISDN—the integrated services digital network protocol for transmitting different digital services through a single channel. In the four years since, an awful lot had changed in both communications technologies and in the world's markets. There was quite a bit of excitement building for the 1991 edition.

The telecom industry had been deregulated in several major countries, leading to a huge increase in the number of customers for suppliers such as Northern, many trying to gain a competitive advantage by rolling out the most advanced technologies as quickly as possible. The establishment of the single European market was just a year away, new markets in Eastern Europe had suddenly opened up with the collapse of the Soviet Union, and the Asia-Pacific region was becoming more closely integrated within an industry that was largely domestic not long ago but was now increasingly global.

On the technology side, while wireless had shot into some prominence, the major focus of Telecom '91 would be the provision of broadband services, with all that implied for fiber optics, the developing standards for synchronous optical transmission, asynchronous transfer mode (ATM) platforms, and more manageable and efficient high-speed fiber networks. The entire event was shaping up to play to our strengths.

Our design called for a two-story air-conditioned pavilion exhibit with the front of the pavilion featuring a 70-foot curved screen for viewing a multilingual video from either the floor or a bridge walkway above and with elaborate working product demonstrations inside. We arranged to have 300 hotel rooms for staff and customer guests, 30 limousines booked for executive and customer use, and the theatre of the Geneva Noga Hilton Hotel booked for 10 days, although we were only putting on one concert by Wynton Marsalis.

I was summoned to a command performance in front of Paul Stern and his executive council to set out my plans. With confidence that everything was covered in advance, the presentation went well until Paul interrupted with, "Who made the goddamn decision to book the theatre for 10 days when we only need it for one night?" Hoping he was in a good mood, I explained that I had learned from a reliable source that two of our major competitors, AT&T and Alcatel, were each planning an event for the theatre and that I'd decided to block them out of it for the run of the show. He seemed to appreciate the feint. The program and budget were approved. As the meeting ended, he said, "Tyson, it better work. Because if you're one Swiss franc over budget, your next job will be taking tickets at the theatre." I think he was smiling.

Building on the networking theme, everything progressed smoothly with two exceptions. First, discovering our pavilion air conditioning couldn't handle the load because of the extreme heat generated in the hall by other exhibitors' equipment and lighting, we negotiated with Palexpo to punch a hole in the roof for outside air (at a cost of more than 100,000 Swiss francs). Second, was finalizing the display graphics and video support for the products. Our exhibit staff was made up of subject matter experts from the various divisions, and each division representative kept bringing forth block network diagrams that connected product architecture to a cloud on top. The graphics were all over the place, with the only common element being a cloud. In exasperation, I finally declared, "No more clouds! Please work something else out." Who would have guessed that 20-odd years later cloud computing would become ubiquitous.

Held under the general theme "An interconnected world: Improving the quality of life for all," Telecom '91 broke all records for the number of both exhibitors (more than 800 from 36 countries) and visitors (about a quarter-million). The event brought together the leaders of the world's telecom industry; system and service providers; decision-makers from industry, finance, banking, and business services; and representatives of governments, operating agencies, regulatory bodies, and user groups.

Ian Craig had given me advice and many helpful tips about managing the production, schooling me in a lot of do's and don'ts. Arriving in Geneva, I remembered his advice that no matter what, I must have one driver and car for my exclusive use at all times. He also suggested that I make sure to pick up the core executives personally and ensure their successful check-in, which the pinstripes couldn't be expected to be able to do on their own.

My driver, a laid-off Swiss banker driving to help a friend, was terrific. My first executive pickup, vice-chairman Dave Vice, arrived on a commercial flight and informed me on the way from the airport that his retirement would soon be announced. Later that day, I greeted Paul Stern and Ed Lucente and their wives who arrived in the corporate Gulfstream jet. Tired and probably regretting not taking the alternative of a first-class commercial flight, they proceeded to debate who got which car. Tipped off in advance to this potential kerfuffle, we had contracted Interpol-sanctioned drivers, a German for Stern and an Italian for Lucente. I followed them to the hotel to make sure they checked in. Oh, the joys of pinstripe egos.

The day before opening, we held a cocktail reception for all executives and their spouses in the entrance lobby to the Noga Hilton Theatre, with the intention of transporting everyone to the convention hall via luxury buses to preview the exhibit, and to use the august crowd as players in a dress rehearsal for the staff. At the reception, Paul Stern, sitting on a sofa with his VP of corporate relations, called me over. "Tyson, why am I in a goddamn junior suite in this hotel?"

I replied, "Sir, you are only staying two nights and if I provided a full suite, it required a minimum ten-day booking. Sorry, but I'm determined to come in not one Swiss franc over budget." He acknowledged my reasoning with a grin and we headed to the buses.

The entire event went off smoothly with only one glaring glitch. In co-operation with the Canadian pavilion, located directly behind our space, we arranged for our scheduled visit with the very important Chinese government delegation to immediately follow their visit to Canada's exhibit. With our executive group standing by to welcome them, the head of the Canadian government pavilion forgot to escort the group to our site, simply watching as the Chinese wandered off to locations unknown.

Protocols and other niceties being what they were among the Chinese, this was a diplomatic disaster of great proportion. Charlie Shiu, our long-standing market-building champion for China who had been developing personal bonds and relationships there for years, jumped to the rescue. He understood the importance of saving face. He handed me 50 of his Chinese business cards and asked me to deliver a bottle of Johnnie Walker Scotch whisky to each delegate's hotel room, accompanied by a personal letter of apology for failing to meet them at the Canadian pavilion. He went off to write the letter and I went off to visit the governmental Canadians with a proposal to salvage the sensitive situation they had created. The next day, after arriving at the Canadian pavilion, the Chinese delegation was formally, and with great fanfare, escorted to our pavilion by the Canadian minister of communications and two RCMP officers in scarlet tunics and Stetsons. Crisis resolved.

Telecom '91 was a success by any measure, including coming in under budget, in large part thanks to the examples set by people such as my operations director who managed everything from the pavilion to our command centre, the controller who also became our limousine fleet dispatcher, and my driver, Jean, who bought 50 bottles of Scotch and delivered them to the Chinese delegation with great dispatch and grace. He even found a lost member of our U.K. board of directors in downtown Geneva at two in the morning and delivered him to his hotel in Montreux, France.

We had a lot fun and, at the end of the show, I hosted a terrific party for more than a hundred staff who stayed to the end, then sent them successfully on their way back to company divisions around the world. Unfortunately, my controller and operations director needed to stay behind for a week to pay all the bills and, looking ahead to Telecom '95, book 300 rooms and negotiate a contract for the Noga Hilton theatre.

As Dave Vice hoped, the perception of Northern Telecom as primarily a North American switch manufacturer soon faded. Northern's huge success with Digital World and OPEN World had been confirmed by growth in market share and profitability, and FiberWorld was widely seen and accepted as a natural extension of our leadership. The impact was substantial. Observing the traffic through our pavilion compared to the traffic volume at the nearby AT&T, Alcatel, Ericsson, Siemens, and Fujitsu pavilions, I could safely say we scared the hell out of our global competitors. At Telecom '91, Northern Telecom emerged as a global power.

For me, Geneva marked the end of an era. I had reached a crossroad. As far back as Digital World, Northern had been an event driven company, as first recognized by Derek Davies. Time and again I had proven the point because the events became benchmark references in corporate history. The work was challenging and fun to do, and I loved the creative space and the learning. What could be more fun than seeing big ideas come to fruition? And there was tremendous satisfaction in sharing the success with those who had committed their heart and soul to the endeavor. But it did take a toll.

After doing it a few times, I had to ask, now what? What was the relevance? Where was the personal fulfillment? Throughout my career I never had aspirations for general management. I hated bureaucratic processes and chasing budgets. I was a content and product guy. To me, the product was always the hero. Product was about making the cash register ring relative to the competition. Reflecting on what came next, I rediscovered that, for me, personal fulfillment was not defined by corporate success but by family. While this might be seen as a profound insight into the blazingly obvious, the rediscovery is better late than never.

So my career as a staff guy in marketing and market development, and as an executive producer in event management came to an end. Left with only the one job of VP of corporate design, my quest for personal fulfillment continued with a long flight back to Ottawa, home to my family, and home to BNR.

8 REDESIGNING ROLES

The adage says "you can never go back," but that wasn't the case with me. Returning to my purple roots in BNR as vice president of corporate design seemed like a natural extension of everything I had learned and done, the cumulative value of my adventures to that point. Management agreed that the industrial design function needed to be rejuvenated and applied across the corporation if Northern wanted to maintain industry leadership in digital communications, and management decided that I was the guy to do it. In addition to being a member of the BNR cabinet reporting to president George Smyth, I also had a Northern Telecom corporate-wide mandate.

I was happy to be back in Ottawa with the Design Interpretive staff. My appointment was well received. I was excited and delighted by the potential for personal fulfillment the new position offered. My ambitions had never encompassed acquiring power—I always defined my adventures by relevance and fulfillment and defined my career in terms of accountability, being acknowledged, then getting on with the job—but being empowered to recreate and reshape the design function held out the prospect of exciting times ahead.

To some, it seemed unusual to have the corporate-wide design function within the research-and-development unit rather than, say, manufacturing, but there was no debate about our group staying within BNR. R&D was the right place for design because the culture of R&D has a longer planning horizon, tolerates more eccentricity, has different criteria for hiring, and has different values for nurturing and developing resources. We were going to make the most of it.

My first act was to create a meaningful corporate design policy and to ratify it with George Smyth and Paul Stern, who was now chairman. I wanted certain things to be set down on paper. We developed a one-page policy statement, signed by Paul and George, which validated the now formally named Corporate Design Group (CDG)'s status as a corporate centre of excellence responsible for driving design excellence and continuity across all Northern products. It acknowledged that my group had signoff authority at all gate reviews in the new product introduction process, and that it was on par with product marketing and product development in contributing to new product definition, conceptualization, specification, and final design. Included in the policy was the creation of a Corporate Design Council to be chaired by Stern and subject to semi-annual review. I insisted on the Council, knowing it would never actually meet—I never called or needed a meeting—because the policy gave me permission to be my own mentor and patron simultaneously.

The policy was really a tool for achieving corporate design leadership, which was my non-negotiable top priority. I had to be able to say that the design process across the company would be guided by design principles based on user values, a view that wasn't always well understood in the higher reaches of the company. We designed to value, not to form. Our core competence was understanding user and chooser values. Our view was outside in. The three key design principles guiding all our work were profound simplicity, conspicuous customer value, and self-evident operation, all aimed at making Northern's products simple to learn and easy to use.

In my first three months back at DI, my senior managers and I worked through a radical reset of the design function. The first step was firmly establishing the Centre of Excellence concept. It was more than just a name. In my view, a Centre of Excellence emerged from the convergence of accountability, value, and leadership. As a centre of excellence, we were accountable for the value we contributed to the corporation. The design policy concentrated on what we could give. Corporate Design made itself accountable for delivering a leadership focus and a strategic force for the drive to industry leadership.

To be in a support or service role is to not be accountable. If you're a support function, you shouldn't be surprised to find people selling or acting in a reactive way. I never liked working in a reactive, responsive mode. I found my way into R&D because I wanted to be at the leading edge of product development, not at the trailing edge or in rescuing mode. The focus of the new design unit would be seeking out opportunities to leverage our talents as essential resources in defining the next generation of communications products.

Switching the mental paradigm of the group was as important as changing institutional realities. Switching the mental paradigm also meant I had to change the name of the organization. Design Interpretive was superseded by the Corporate Design Group (CDG). It was hard for me to let the old name go, but the metamorphosis was what mattered. Figuring we had to say goodbye to say hello, I asked DI staff to create a time capsule for burial and invited DI alumnae to a special ceremony. Many who had retired or left came back or sent artifacts. With pizza for lunch, we gathered in the main inner courtyard for the internment ceremony, complete with eulogies to celebrate the life of DI. We turned over some sod, formally said good-bye to Design Interpretive, and then had a wake for 150 people at my house. We had a contest for the best limerick to go on a memorial plaque on the nearest lab wall. The winner, Chris White, wrote:

The folks in DI had great arts
And a vast array of talents and smarts
We formed an oasis
Where fine interfaces
Brought joy to our minds and our hearts.

DI was dead. Long live CDG.

The event also set what I thought was the right tone for the group, underlining the notion that we needed to have fun. Accordingly, reminiscent of the early years when we closed DI offices to give the staff a break from the day-to-day churn of work in progress, we implemented quarterly group information sessions (GIS) with the simple objective of sharing what we were doing. We held each half-day GIS in the Ottawa auditorium with real time private corporate video links to our offices in Harlow and Calgary (amazing for its time). The program reviews quickly became laugh-filled events that included costumes and comedy skits. Formerly dull and boring reviews became team events that built the spirit of the whole organization. Over time, an expected final feature of every GIS was one employee's Letterman-style top ten list. More often than not, I was the butt of the jokes.

In line with my longstanding campaign, I was determined to change thinking about design as an expense to thinking about it as an investment, just as I had in the corporate marketing culture. Changing the funding mechanism was essential, so I got Paul and George to invert our funding model. It was an easy sell.

DI had been set up to sell the function to various groups within Northern as a competitive edge for the work they wanted done. We had been funded at the bottom as subcontractors. Having an organization funded on subcontracts was fundamentally wrong. As a centre of excellence, we invested in our partners rather than being hired by them. Designers usually spent most of their time selling the value of design, but we were in control and couldn't be going out with a tin cup. Instead, we would go to a meeting with product managers and say, "I'm not here to get money. I'm here to invest in your future." I told everyone to stop selling. I struck the words 'client' and 'selling' from the vocabulary and insisted on using 'partner', which lined up well with the investment concept. Those partnership investments could take the form of defining user requirements, design evaluation, user-interaction design, visual-interface design, industrial design, graphic design, mechanical design, and prototype development and transfer.

We established a corporate-funded budget for CDG of about 1 percent of R&D. The significance was not in the amount of funding (it was about a 10 percent increase) but that the certainty of multi-year funding at a specific percentage of the overall budget allowed us to align our human resources with future-oriented programs. Rather than a consistently underfunded budget of negotiated bits and pieces, our budget and program were presented and approved as a whole. The effect was that we truly did become investors in the divisions' products. In the division guys' perception, they saved money.

I committed our group to forging—and continually renewing—a clear vision of how our product base was likely to change. We were committed to being the first to identify the power shifts that were discontinuous with existing groups of products, businesses, technologies, and ways of thinking, shifts that would reshape the customer's definition of value. BNR and Northern had done that before, several times, and we were determined to do it again.

My focus was on allocating CDG's resources to projects oriented toward creating future value. While I was also responsible for the design work going on in labs in Europe, Asia, and elsewhere around the world, most of that work was sustaining development and could be monitored in program reviews, allowing the Ottawa group to do the original work concentrating on new and exploratory products.

My major intervention in the three-month reset process came when various organizational structures and processes were being tossed around for discussion. I told management to stop talking and let the structure follow from what we decided about the program. Program should always precede structure.

We decided that CDG's value lay in working horizontally across the business units, both from the standpoint of bringing continuity to products and of generating power shifts. We analyzed Northern's entire operation from the design perspective and created five core programs that cut across the businesses, treating them as focal points for both continuity and defining future value.

I wanted to change how our business partners thought about and deployed their resources. I wanted to break out of the patterns of R&D investment that concentrated on sustaining platforms and focus instead on new generation and vision platforms. We reconfigured our investments, shifting from 80 percent investment in current products that were proven earners, to 80 percent in new generation and vision platforms. By choosing how we would invest in our partners' programs, we influenced them toward greater investment in the future, with development teams each working on a particular line—current, new generation, and vision. Similarly, we set up product design managers to be accountable for a set of products, such as terminals, also on only one line: current, new generation, or vision. Design now faced outward by product instead of by function, as it had in DI.

I adapted an oil-industry methodology for creating new product concepts. Analysis, extrapolation, and being logical all involve one type of thinking. Forecasting by extrapolation can give you the "ers"—faster, cheaper, smaller, stronger—but can't give you a new concept. Different approaches were required to challenge the obvious and get to the next level. I believed power shifts demanded backcasting, postulating future power shifts and interpolating back to the present. If you jump to the future and work your way back, the solution will be different than if you start in the present and keep moving forward. Interpolating from the future to the present changes your viewpoint. Such jumps are not logical. They only appear that way after the fact.

The focus on accountability for adding value paid off. One product manager stopped work on two products under development because they weren't sufficiently visionary. If he'd been in service mode, he might not have bothered, thinking that coming up with the overall definition of the product wasn't his job. Now he had to question whether the product could take us into the future. Rejecting the old design led to a cross-functional team exploring and defining value from the customer's point of view. The result was the design of a new modular phoneset, the Vista 250/350 terminal introduced in 1994.

The telecommunications industry was undergoing such turmoil and churn that there were abundant opportunities to develop future-oriented products—especially for Northern since we were leading the industry in so many market categories.

One area where we were not leading the industry was in wireless technologies. We weren't even participating in that market segment as it evolved in the 1980s. But John Roth, in charge of product-line management after leaving the presidency of BNR in 1986, convinced Paul Stern that wireless networks were rolling out so quickly and the number of mobile customers expanding so rapidly that cellular networks, still analog, would have to become digital. Then the value in those networks would shift from radio technologies, the strong suit of the industry leaders, to switching between cells. Demand for new and more powerful switches would inevitably and dramatically rise. They did and, to his credit, Roth had the wireless systems group up and running by 1991.

Motorola and Ericsson were the world's wireless leaders and John negotiated a joint venture with Motorola—a marriage of convenience, really—to buy some time and some access to Motorola's radio expertise. Soon after, Northern bought the cellular division of Novatel in Calgary, setting up a wireless development centre there, then formed a strategic alliance with Matra Communications in France. Northern also took a minority interest in Matra as an important player in Europe's wireless market. Within five years, the wireless business accounted for about 15 percent of Northern's revenues.

Once again a product guy, I soon discovered the unrelenting pressure we were under to reduce expenses. Faced with uncontrolled global expansion resulting from product success, Stern was hammering for expense reductions wherever he could find them. Operations reviews became inquisitions. Senior people were retiring, losing their jobs, or otherwise leaving the company. Previously hairline cracks began to open, resulting in a cultural change where power and control rather than collaboration began to dominate. It didn't help that we were in the middle of a global recession and our major customers were holding back the capital investment required to build out their networks.

Stern was doing his job, however, whether we liked it or not, and deserved credit for improving the company's financial performance. In an environment where cash is king, every one and every thing is an expense. In a world where negative cash flow is a crisis, short-term expediency will displace the long-term integrity of leading-edge research every time. Product development groups forced to hang on and not allowed to defer schedules will take the only option available. They'll defer the future and hope they can catch up later. In a business world without choice, that's not a villain vs. victim scenario, just reality.

Within our sphere of reality, the spirit of optimism remained. We were always driven by our vision, passion, and commitment and by our proven ability to execute the promise. We got on with the job. My greatest concern was falling one step behind. I had seen Digital Equipment consumed by Hewlett-Packard, Rolm by IBM, and STC by Northern. All had fallen one step behind and, shifting from proactive to reactive modes, had failed to adapt to changing market realities. In my experience, corporations that fail to continuously innovate are vulnerable to product atrophy or being made obsolete by competition. Innovate or die is the stuff of entire libraries of academic case studies.

At CDG, we played our part in driving innovation at Northern, developing a predictive portfolio of prototypes whose innovative values and features cascaded into many new products. One concept focused on multimedia messaging and integrated management of voice, fax, and video mailboxes. The modular Vista family of terminals incorporated many of its design factors. Another concept focused on using calling line identification and other information to help manage communications. Many of those functions were incorporated in both the Maestro and Nomad cordless phones—the first to have on-screen features in the handset—and in the Companion digital cordless phone for the business market, which let PBX users roam their workplaces. A favourite concept was called Orbitor, which in its earliest days was a small, lightweight mobile pager and voice device that allowed users to both read messages and to write messages on the screen with a stylus and send them.

In the early nineties, however, constrained by the global recession and with an unrelenting focus on the "D" in R&D, we had reluctant partners in our network-centric culture. We needed to get senior management to buy into our work, so we packaged some of the items in our predictive terminal portfolio as VFT-1 (Very Fast Track or, as it was known internally, Venus Fly Trap) to present to Paul Stern whenever we could catch his attention.

Hard to track down or get a meeting with, I discovered that Stern was coming to Ottawa for a half-day visit with various managers in the spring of 1992. Determined to get at least a half-hour of his time, I verified his schedule and put a plan in place. I had our contract limo service bring the stretch limo they would assign to him to the labs for my designers to measure the back seat space, including the drive shaft hump. We created a custom-designed black display shelf and prepared a VFT-1 portfolio that included Orbitor, Vista, and SoundBeam, a personal, wearable speakerphone with magical acoustic technology that elicited "must-have" responses from trial users.

I watched Paul arrive from my ground floor office window near the entrance. He came straight from the lobby and walked into my office saying, "So, what's new?" I offered to show him what was new on the way to the airport, hoping I would be the only passenger. He took the bait and went off to his meetings on-site. We gave ourselves one hour to set up the display in the limo, just in case he got through the meetings quickly and left early. His meetings over on schedule, he and I headed to the private terminal at the airport while I did my song and dance in the cramped quarters of the limo. He invited me to continue the conversation on the corporate jet—insisted actually—so I boarded his plane and flew to Toronto while the driver took the predictive products back to the lab. I later caught a commercial flight back to Ottawa. The meeting resulted in a connection to Matra for the first Northern Telecom cell phone and the prototype development of Orbitor.

We prepared another demonstration of the predictive products for a meeting of the board of directors at Ottawa's BNR headquarters in October 1992. As always at board meetings, the executive committee wielding the real power met off on their own while other members otherwise filled their time. In what I often suspected was the need to fill an agenda while the real power met, I was frequently pulled in to talk to—that is, to entertain—various subcommittees of the board. I took no offense. Being free of complex technology and jargon, my presentations had human interest and great visuals and, because the products were easy to relate to, board members, as users themselves, felt an opportunity to offer their opinions and to influence the company's direction.

Always good fun for me, over the years I was able to meet a wonderful cross section of successful people that included former Canadian provincial premiers, former U.S. cabinet secretaries and state governors, a celebrity broadcaster, diplomats, and former CEOs. Some were very impressive people, some very much less so. The mystery that prevailed throughout my career was what value the board members not on the executive committee brought to the table in terms of content or understanding our business beyond some apparent value in having access to political and business elites.

On the day of the board meeting, my staff set up the demo in a secure area on the mezzanine floor of the campus conference centre where the board met. The board members came to experience our new products, some by invitation, some by just strolling over after the meeting broke up into small groups. I joined the rest of the BNR cabinet for morning coffee with Stern and Ed Lucente. There were rumours that Stern, now chairman and CEO, was going to use the meeting to anoint Lucente as president and his likely successor. By midday, I began to notice executives who rarely came to the labs wandering around with nervous looks on their faces. I heard that the corporate fleet of aircraft had been in the air overnight and through the morning.

About four o'clock, I returned to the conference centre to remove the exhibit and thank my staff. Unaware of what had gone on during the day, I looked down into the lobby and will never forget the sight of a grim-faced Stern and Lucente storming toward the front entrance and their waiting cars. I soon learned that core North American executives had been quietly summoned to attend a reception at the Chateau Laurier Hotel downtown where the executive committee introduced Bell Canada's chairman and CEO, Jean Monty, as Northern's new president and chief operating officer. What some described as a *coup d'etat* was performed with surgical precision, the move protected by the exclusiveness and privacy of the executive committee. Any second-guessing was left to industry pundits and the media.

I learned later that customers' complaints about Stern were one of the key factors in the board's decision. The DMS family of switches was the biggest revenue generator for Northern in the late 1980s and early 1990s. We'd sold thousands of them around the world and, as the product evolved, so many lines of software code were added—more than 20 million—that software reliability became an issue with major customers. Some switches even crashed. Stern was so busy concentrating on controlling expenses, expanding overseas, and ensuring short-term profitability that he seemed at best lackadaisical in addressing the problem and some customers, especially Bell South, complained directly to Bell Canada. Northern reached back into the parent company for stability and continuity, just as it had with Bob Scrivener and Walter Light.

In a press release announcing Monty's appointment as president, Stern said, "We are fortunate to attract to the presidency of Northern Telecom an executive of Mr. Monty's high caliber and broad experience in the telecommunications industry. He is an important addition to our senior management team." A few months later, having left the company along with Ed Lucente, Stern was quoted in a U.S. business magazine saying, "Nobody's going to shove a president down my throat."

Jean Monty's appointment as CEO in the spring of 1993 also came with a fundamental change in corporate governance in line with a private industry trend at the time forced by shareholder pressure. The new rule required a non-executive chairman elected from among the outside directors. Monty was still a member of the board but was free to address the priorities of the economy and the market, while the chairman took care of the board members and their committees. It was a useful buffer as Monty toured the world getting back into customers' good graces.

My first introduction to him came when he visited BNR headquarters in Ottawa for an in-depth overview of the company's activities. As a cabinet member, I presented on behalf of my Corporate Design Group and expected an in-depth discussion about product to follow, but Monty focused on his long-standing admiration for the BNR corporate identity and its vision statement. The discussion was enlightening and revealed his personal values. Even more gratifying, one of his first acts was to reverse the treatment of R&D as an expense and publicly declare it an investment.

Jean had many of the attributes of Ed Fitzgerald. He was a consummate gentleman, a team-builder, and a listener who embraced the corporate culture. But the company he inherited was huge and suffering from all the natural strains and stresses that come with growth and great success. The corporate culture had changed dramatically during Stern's tenure, from one based on trust to one concentrated on power and control. The corporate vision was battered and bruised. Jean's management style was dramatically different than Stern's. Rather than exercise control and direction from the top, he listened carefully, pulled on his key resources, and sought consensus. In personal skills, he was best in class.

Coming from a career as Northern's major customer, he loved being with other customers and they loved working with him because he shared their values and could speak their language. Though not a product guy, Jean was a people person as well as a customer champion. To him, raising the level of customer satisfaction was a top priority and "putting the customer first" was the first rule of customer satisfaction. To highlight his passion, he created dozens of programs and initiatives to define a customer-first culture and a CEO's Customer First Awards program that was featured at annual sales and senior management conferences.

With a similar focus on employee satisfaction, he travelled extensively throughout the company, holding town halls and listening to employees' views, hopes, and complaints. He wanted to boost morale and build support for the many changes he was making and, with his admiration for BNR's identity and tradition, he invited me to work with him to craft statements defining a new spirit, corporate mission, and core values. Convincing Jean that brand identity was more than just share of mind and also meant share of heart, I reintroduced him to the vision statement I'd worked on with Don Chisholm more than 20 years earlier for the launch of BNR. He liked it, and adding only one word—leadership— the vision was repositioned as *The Spirit of Northern Telecom* preceding the core values and introduced to employees at a senior management conference in March 1994.

I enjoyed working with him from the beginning because of his great sense of humour, his desire to listen, and the high value questions he asked. He loved being around R&D types and bringing global customers to the labs. Challenged with a company that now operated in 90 countries, with over 60,000 employees, he reached beyond his direct reports. He liked to informally network with opinion leaders, while being careful not to bypass organizational protocol.

He had a big mess to clean up, especially with the global economy still in recession and customers still angry about software glitches. Northern lost more than a billion dollars in the second quarter of 1993 alone and lost almost half its stock market value in just a few weeks. In June of that year, Monty announced that Northern would take a huge restructuring charge to cover the cost of fixing the software, shed about 10 percent of its employees, and close several facilities. The company posted a full-year loss of $884 million, but he at least successfully soothed customer anxiety by committing $250 million to rewriting and simplifying the switching software by the end of 1995. He also upped the R&D budget to just over 11 percent of revenue, still below traditional levels but almost a full percentage point over what Paul Stern devoted to the future. In 1992, Northern Telecom invested over $1 billion in research and development work by BNR, despite the massive losses.

Then, to address the organization's size and complexity, Monty implemented huge structural changes to Northern's business model and to BNR. Characteristic of CEOs entering a new corporate culture, Monty reached back to his old company for people he trusted. At the end of June 1993, he appointed Brian Hewat as chairman and chief executive officer of BNR, both new positions since BNR had never had anyone but a president in charge. Brian had spent decades at Bell Canada in senior marketing positions before becoming president and CEO of the Stentor Resource Centre alliance of Canada's nine major telecom operating companies.

In the announcement, Monty said, "Our rapid expansion, as well as the internationalization of the telecom industry, makes it necessary for us to continue to build the management strength of BNR." Responsibilities were divvied up. BNR already had about 10,000 employees after the expansion in the United Kingdom and the Asia/Pacific region in the previous few years, and planned to hire many more. President George Smyth would focus on BNR's core technologies and the international expansion strategy, while Brian would direct the product groups and associated administrative functions. Northern was on a quest for growth from geographic diversity and positioning BNR in Europe, Japan, China, and Australia was seen as a key element.

BNR, rather than being decentralized was, in corporate-speak, "globalized" to be closer to the market and to the customers the labs served, which had been the case and strength of BNR from the very beginning. BNR was always customer-centric. From the creation of an R&D division headquartered in Ottawa, each Northern division had a lab and R&D director, and the labs expanded alongside the customer base.

Raleigh's Research Triangle Park campus in North Carolina became the center of the great switching juggernaut, taking over from the switching division in Bramalea, Ontario that first made analog switches under license from Western Electric and then manufactured the DMS portfolio. The transmission division that established its headquarters in Atlanta was supported by associated manufacturing and R&D from Lachine, Quebec. The Belleville lab, home of PBX and business terminals, expanded to Mountain View, California, while London's station apparatus facility expanded to Nashville, Tennessee. With Northern finally getting out of the gate in the wireless field, the wireless network group became centred in Richardson, Texas with support from the Calgary facility. Switching and transmission retained their names over time, but the PBX and station apparatus divisions became "enterprise." With acquisitions along the way and with one begetting another, labs emerged all over the world, in China, the U.K., France, Australia, Germany, India, Russia, and the Middle East.

Through it all, the Ottawa campus remained the jewel in the crown, the mecca for customers looking for the reassurance of a safe buy from a leading supplier who would be around for the long term and also looking for a pretty good time. While BNR president John Roth was better as a host than main performer, most comfortable addressing business details and drawing on R&D experts critical to a sale, Don Chishlom, with his laid-back style and intellect, and George Smyth, with his spirit, passion, and commitment, became part of BNR folklore—like DI's beanbag chairs and maybe even me. It was often said visitors didn't understand anything Don and George said, but just loved the way they said it.

The tours in Ottawa never stopped. In the early days, things were fairly simple. Entering the front administration building, visitors went into the auditorium just off the lobby to meet and greet the lab and other executives and were then taken on a walkabout. Two features then could impress anyone. The first was the computer room on the first floor of Lab 2 enclosed with large glass windows. Visitors could view the latest IBM computers and staff loading giant disc drives while high-speed printers spewed out reams of paper printouts from punch code cards deposited by engineers and scientists. The second was the custom-wafer silicon lab on the second floor of Lab 1. Visitors could see technicians in white suits and hats working in the state-of-the-art clean room fabricating custom chips for Digital World products. Some thought the staff looked like creatures from space, though I always thought they looked like sperm. As the labs grew and the number of visits increased so dramatically, we had to design and build demonstration displays to heighten the value of the walkabouts and further impress the guests, both customers and the world's grand pooh-bahs who also came in droves.

The Shah of Iran made the first royal visit to the Ottawa headquarters, before my time and before BNR. While Don Chisholm was president, we had a visit from the USSR's leader, Leonid Brezhnev. After then recent uprisings in the Eastern bloc, we had lots of accomplished researchers and engineers from countries such as Hungary, Romania, and Poland who weren't thrilled about the visit. With everyone in the government concerned with security and protests, Don, in his typical common-sense style, simply issued a memo inviting anyone who disdained the pending visit to take the day off. On the day of Brezhnev's tour, security included an armed motorcade, armed security on the rooftops, and dozens of plainclothes RCMP and Soviet agents. The day went off without incident.

I have especially fond memories of a visit by Sweden's King Carl Gustaf because it was so out of the ordinary by VIP standards. As the honourary head of the Royal Swedish Academy of Sciences, he quietly joined Academy members for a non-state visit to Canada. The Academy requested a low-key visit to BNR, diplomatic protocol being what it was. But before the federal government was finished, the visit included a state dinner, hosted by the Governor-General, with a couple of hundred ministers, pinstripes, and high-level bureaucrats in attendance. As official BNR host, I was invited to the dinner and assigned to a table at the back of the room where I joined the King's personal bodyguard and the senior

RCMP assigned to the delegation. We had a lot more fun than most of the other tables.

The visit that got the most news coverage was Russian president Boris Yeltsin's tour of Lab 5 in June 1992 almost a year before its official opening. Yeltsin arrived in the wobbling state seen on many of his other public engagements. He was jovial, engaging, and well received by the audience. During the welcome, he picked up a revolutionary surface-emitting laser microchip BNR had just announced, looked carefully at it, and made a motion to put it in the inside pocket of his suit jacket. Not missing a beat, our host, George Smyth, sternly mimed Boris to give it back, which he did with feigned reluctance to gales of laughter and applause. I remember the visit best for inviting the CDG staff that had designed and built the displays and the corporate relations staff who had worked so hard to organize the event for pizza and beer at my home after work. BNR security later expressed some frustration that a large banner that read "Welcome" in Russian had disappeared. It was hanging from the eaves of my house to welcome our guests (and is still in my garage).

The visits became a little more low-key after George, as the architect of BNR's globalization, relocated to London in 1994. Brian Hewat was not, by nature, as demonstrative a character as either George or Don. A classic pinstripe, he was a gracious host to all visitors, refined, diplomatic, and always dressed to the nines. He also smoked a pipe and I joined him, often daily, in the underground garage for a smoke and rants about areas of mutual concern.

In those informal get-togethers, I discovered he loved playing piano and had a great sense of humour, which stood me in good stead when he needed a new office on the executive top floor of our Ottawa tower next to my humble digs, the two glass-enclosed offices separated by a corridor. I arrived one morning to find a clear glass entrance door to the hallway had been installed, complete with a sign featuring Brian's name and title. I was now at the end of his custom-enclosed corridor. While he was out of town, I arranged to have a sign installed on his side of the door, reading "John Tyson, Vice-President Corporate Design Group." Startled by his first visit to my quarters next door, he entered laughing as I explained how honoured I was that my chairman and CEO had installed a private passageway to my office for quick and easy access.

Six months after Brian took up his duties at BNR, Jean Monty announced his next major reorganization initiative, splitting Northern's management structure into two operating groups. World Trade, led by Jim Long, would oversee all business and marketing activities outside North America. The North American group, headed by John Roth, would oversee global product strategy, product groups, and marketing organizations in Canada and the U.S. Roth's organization was organized on a network group basis, with four lines of business—switching networks, wireless networks, enterprise networks, and broadband networks—serving particular sets of customers. The four network businesses were restructured with presidents in charge.

The changes were extensive over a short period of time and somewhat destabilizing since the organizational changes were accompanied by a recasting of many characters. Des Hudson retired as president of Northern Telecom Europe. Roy Merrills retired as head of the American subsidiary. David Twyver became president of wireless, replacing Roth. My old boss, John Taylor, resigned from the transmission group to create his own venture company. Don Peterson, the group VP for enterprise networks, resigned to join AT&T, later becoming the founding CEO of Avaya. No company can rest on its laurels, but that kind of swift change generates culture shock for any organization. Monty said the changes were designed to prepare Northern to capitalize on new growth opportunities and that, "While 1993 was a tough year, I believe that in many areas of the business we've turned the corner, especially when it comes to product orientation and product development." To everyone's good fortune, as the economy recovered Northern was able to turn its operating loss of $884 million in 1993, into a $404 million profit for 1994.

The restructuring was generally well received by customers, but was worrisome to many of us veteran R&D guys, an ominous sign of things to come. The four BNR VPs in the lines of business (LOBs) now had dual reporting relationships. Each reported to an LOB president and to BNR president George Smyth, who in turn reported to chairman and CEO Brian Hewat who reported to Monty who had no product experience except as a customer. George later remarked that he thought the job of president came with all the levers; the only problem was that they weren't connected to anything. To me, he understated things. It was more like the head was separated from the spinal cord. I always liked the definition of power as the ability to control and assign dollars and/or resources because without it you can only advocate. The convoluted management structure meant that George actually had no power.

John Roth in his new role with global responsibility for "product evolution" had no direct R&D control, even though he actually was in control of product. Evolution, to many of us, implied sustaining development, cost control, and operating effectiveness, not necessarily innovation. Evolution meant doing something better; innovation meant doing something different. On paper, Jean Monty controlled everything, yet to us it seemed he was preparing to give Roth the presidential crown some years down the road. We may have been just lowly R&D VPs, but we understood power. The dual reporting relationships were neither stable nor manageable.

The reorganization complete, Monty next turned to three initiatives designed to redefine the company's role in an ever more tumultuous industry. All centred on the fact that 1995 would mark the company's first hundred years in business. He commissioned renowned Canadian business writer Peter C. Newman to produce a book detailing the company's first century, he set about defining a new vision for the company that would build on the spirit of Digital World, OPEN World, and FiberWorld, and he retained a New York agency to design and implement a new corporate identity.

As it developed, the new vision—A World of Networks—seemed weak to me. It wasn't a product offer like Digital World, OPEN World, or FiberWorld. It was simply a pragmatic description of the global communications environment and what Northern could supply. It wasn't forward looking, nor set any new technological stake in the marketplace. To the New York agency, however, the vision went hand in hand with a new identity built around changing the company name from Northern Telecom to Nortel. The agency designed the "O" in the new shortened name as a global mark that, according to the agency, reinforced the company's identity as a supplier of global networks.

I got an inside tip of what was happening. The corporate VP of marketing invited me to join him in a meeting with Monty where I saw the proposed global mark for the first time. It looked like an astrolabe. As an exercise in graphic design, the work to date to me did not reflect the culture of the organization or its values and spirit.

Known only to a very few, I worked up a counter proposal for the new identity that added the BNR icon to embrace the entire company, partly in an effort to make sure the icon was embedded in the corporate name, but also because I thought it conveyed a natural evolution of the spirit and values and of what we had accomplished together. The proposal even abandoned purple, which broke my heart, but I was trying to enhance the new Nortel identity with what I believed would be an everyone-wins scenario.

I presented the ideas to a set of top executives, including Monty and Roth, who instructed me to take the solution as a done deed to the corporate relations group working with the New York agency. Unfortunately, at the eleventh hour, it was sabotaged by a piece of spurious research, hastily done via brand-equity focus groups in Europe, which confirmed that the icon had no brand equity. Any fool familiar with market research would know that the BNR icon would have low brand equity when shown in association with Nortel, a name that did not yet exist in the market, and when there had been zero marketing investment to burn the brand. Just days before I was to make a presentation to the board of directors' executive committee, I was told my proposal was dead. Defeated, I destroyed the presentation material, the only remnant being a set of prototype glass coasters containing the proposed logo and a few black-and-white photos.

Jean Monty specifically asked that I present the spirit, core values, and vision statements to the executive committee and describe all aspects of the program for launching A World of Networks over the coming year, including rollout, event schedules, and media plans. I was to be followed by the VP of marketing who was there to reveal the new corporate identity and design. He never had the chance to get too far into his presentation. The meeting deteriorated into a very heated debate over the name change. Jean diplomatically stopped the proceedings and asked us to withdraw and wait in his office. Some time later he joined us and, ever gracious, apologized for not anticipating the sensitivity of certain members of the executive committee who were displaced by new governance rules adopted by the board earlier in the day.

The new rules no longer allowed past chairmen to sit on the board. As a result, Walter Light and Ed Fitzgerald were out. Walter and Ed argued that the Northern name in various manifestations had worked well for a century so why change it now. I don't think their objections had much to do with the name. They had just been kicked off the board and were offended. The meeting is hard to forget, as it was the last time I met with the two men.

I can only assume the meeting was a courtesy and the name change didn't require board approval because the new name was announced in April 1995 at the annual general meeting, held in Montreal where the company had been founded a hundred years before. As Peter Newman put it in his centennial history, "Monty used the meeting... to announce that the tradition, the memories and the century-old equity in the Northern name were being retained in the legal name of the corporation: Northern Telecom. But, henceforth, throughout the world, the company would be known by its new logo: Nortel."

That was all well and good, but all the PR bullshit got under my skin from the beginning. As a product guy, I wanted to know where we were going on a much more specific basis. As Brian Hewat pointed out in 1995, 80 percent of Nortel's revenues came from products and services BNR had developed within the previous five years. By year's end, we had 15,000 people working in almost 30 labs in 13 countries. We had received a technology boost and gained some competitive advantages by forming alliances and joint ventures with partners in India, Turkey, Austria, France, and Germany. We had eight joint ventures in China alone.

With increased investment in wireless, enterprise, and broadband networks, R&D spending in 1995 reached $1.6 billion, 14.8 percent of revenues. But what were we doing with it? Thankfully, there was still some leading-edge product in the pipeline, including the Magellan product line of broadband multimedia products that had been rolling out since the early nineties, with the Passport enterprise switch, Gateway carrier access switch, and the Concorde backbone network switch. Some exciting innovations in the Ottawa wireless group were generating a broad swath of patents.

But the combination of massive increases in development resources and global market expansion consumed everyone and every dollar at the expense of exploratory research. The four presidents of the lines of business took control of R&D, forcing their R&D vice presidents into those dual reporting relationships, reporting to both the LOB president and the chairman and president of BNR. With more than 85 percent of the funding now under the control of the LOB presidents, the BNR vice-presidents became *de facto* staff guys. Product was now controlled within the silo of each independent line of business. Sustaining development became the priority over advanced technology.

We now faced LOBs as global profit centers with the presidents reporting to Monty. Meanwhile, Roth, also reporting to Monty, controlled operations and had global responsibility for product evolution. It was like the Abbott and Costello who's-on-first skit. The answer was no one. Monty owned the corporate vision. Nobody owned the product innovation challenge that would create the next discontinuity. Partitioned for effectiveness and efficiency within each product group, the complex matrix started to kill BNR, the goose that had laid the golden eggs for Northern for 20 years.

The credo changed from a longstanding bet-the-business stance, to a protect-the-business environment. From aspiring to technology leadership, the desire diminished to one of managing the program. Demand for current product still exceeded supply, so the focus was on producing better, faster, smarter, and building corporate capacity to meet the surging demand.

What was concerning to some of us wasn't so much our inability to change the dominant network-centric view, it was the dramatic shift in power and control and the neutralizing of the front-end exploratory research. I knew we were in trouble when R&D product strategy was suddenly driven by the need to create a consistent message for the centennial celebrations and for Telecom '95 coming up in Geneva in October.

Always the classic event-driven company, Northern once again rallied the troops around the obvious event of its centennial, then discovered that would not bring in a single new customer or sell a single new product. It had been years since FiberWorld and competition was heating up, exemplified by the likes of Cisco, Nokia, and Motorola. Telecom '95 was a timely international venue to raise the corporate profile. The problem was what to say.

I thought I'd finished my extended sojourn in event marketing when I moved back to Ottawa, but I was pulled back in as Telecom '95 approached. I was already engaged in T '95 on the product innovation side, creating a private backroom in our pavilion, entered by invitation only, to demonstrate our most advanced technologies. That project was well in hand, but the T '95 team was having trouble resolving message content and the collateral material required for distribution at a press conference where Monty, Roth, and Long would unveil the World of Networks vision.

Schedule pressures were unrelenting. Out of loyalty to those who had helped me years before, I was particularly committed to helping Ray Langton, now director of operations for Telecom '95, and Velma Leblanc, the editor of *Telesis*. Ray had been mission critical to the launch of FiberWorld and Telecom '91, and Velma and her team had saved the day with *Telesis* then and on many other occasions. Answering Ray's call for help, I promised to address the exhibit's live product demonstrations on the Palexpo floor and the special edition of *Telesis* planned to mark the 100th anniversary.

With only months to complete the issue, Velma had to call in the resources of more than a hundred people from around the company. With one month to go, the team worked around the clock and brought in freelance writers, copy-editors, proofreaders, and photographers, joined by CDG's graphic designer and *Telesis'* art director. All the articles were being written concurrently and editing for continuity was, to say the least, arduous. It was numbing watching conflicts in R&D strategy resolved by editors, writers, and public relations staff seeking continuity to articles they were feverishly turning out to meet a deadline.

It was unusual for the technical journal to reflect current executives, but the issue featured more than 20 pinstripes as purported authors, supported by wordsmiths and editors. The focus was network carrier-centric to a fault, almost unrelenting in its definition of the customer being the network provider, with the end user merely a connection. Primarily focused on extrapolations of where we were and how well we had done, the issue highlighted current product evolution, market development, and the dollar investment commitment that was yet another extrapolation of our high investment ratio at the time.

It was only at the eleventh hour and in the very last article completed that the word Internet was pulled forward. Being Jean Monty's lead article, it also represented the final editing for continuity across the 180-page hardcover book that was an honest reflection of who we were at the time and our intrinsic values, with a dozen articles and associated box stories. Browsing it almost 20 years later, I could find the term World Wide Web used only once.

Thanks to Velma and her team, the special issue made it on time to a Telecom that was very different from the one four years earlier. The massively increased use of the Internet, mobile communications, and multimedia made those fields much more prominent. The ITU's secretary-general noted that fewer than five million people worldwide were connected to the Internet at the time of Telecom '91 but the number had reached 36 million in the fall of 1995, with about two million more users signing on each month. There was a special weekend session to look at the communications infrastructure that supported the Internet and to address problems in its development.

The secretary-general also noted the spectacular growth of cellular telephone subscribers worldwide from a mere 15 million in 1991 to more than 50 million in 1995, with hundreds of millions more expected in just a few short years. The focus on multimedia, including broadband advances in high-speed ATM transmission and optical switching systems, was sharpened by the number of companies scrambling to get a toehold in the multimedia market. The biggest change on the Palexpo floor to me was the range of companies exhibiting at what had traditionally been a purely telecom industry event. Intel, Microsoft, Oracle, and other software firms were there for the first time. Convergence was all the rage, the trend reflected in the theme of "Connect!"

I spent the night before the opening dry-running our presentation in the invitation-only room for Orbitor, the personal communicator concept designed for multi-tasking. By 1995, Orbitor featured integrated voice and data, a pull-down keyboard, a removable Bluetooth earpiece, a personal directory, text messaging, email, and a touch-sensitive screen. The special *Telesis* issue featured photographs of the product concepts revealed in the private demo room and laid out our guiding principles of design innovation: profound simplicity, self-evidence, and conspicuous customer value. The article also featured six video prototypes created for behavioural research in addition to the physical prototypes, such as the perception analyzer, a research tool that captured moment-by-moment audience reaction to the broadband applications shown. The video prototypes included touch-sensitive, large-screen, colour tablets in medical and domestic applications.

On opening day, while wandering the aisles of Palexpo, I discovered old friends I hadn't seen in a while. Sadly, the list of Nortel executive expatriates was growing. I ran into my old boss from Atlanta, John Taylor, Terry Mathews, and Gerry Butters, our former senior VP of marketing and now president of AT&T network systems' global public networks. John had a booth for his new venture company and Terry was doing what he did best as the front-and-centre figure for Newbridge. Gerry was leading AT&T's contingent. Clearing it with our pavilion director, I invited them to join me for a drink in our hospitality suite, to be joined by Ian Craig and Dave Twyver. Other executives seeing competitors in our private bar gave us some puzzled looks, but friendships matter.

At the press conference, Monty told the media that A World of Networks "sets our future direction and positioning as a company that's designing, building and integrating networks for communications, information, entertainment, education and commerce. It's with some hesitation that I call A World of Networks a vision, because it's really no less than a total redefinition of Nortel in terms of our purpose, our products, and our customer base.... This is truly a historic moment for us. We've spent the past year celebrating the company's achievements over the past century. They were significant. Here in Geneva, we're putting the past behind us and facing a new future."

This was all true. But to me, A World of Networks was little more than an extension of promises past and a reassurance of a safe buy to our channel customers; more a position to market than a vision. I believed we needed a declared product vision. A World of Networks was anything but.

The press conference was well attended and generally well received. Later that evening, we held a reception and a private fireworks display we had commissioned on Lake Geneva. Accompanying our guests onto the Noga Hilton Hotel's terrace balcony, I looked below to see my old friend Gerry Butters staring back up at me with a wicked smile. He remembered how an astute Northern sales executive, looking to be a sponsor of the PGA Westchester Open in New York some years earlier, discovered that AT&T had bought the rights to the beer sales and hospitality tents but had neglected to reserve the rights to the plastic containers. Our guy bought those rights, resulting in thousands of golf fans walking around drinking AT&T beer from Northern Telecom cups. Unable to resist the opportunity to reverse the sting, Gerry booked the terrace below for a late-evening reception and invited AT&T's guests to enjoy Northern Telecom's fireworks. Once our customers were put to bed, Yolanda and I arrived at the British pub behind the Hilton for a pint or two to be greeted by Gerry shouting, "Gotcha!"

Telecom '95 was a successful event. Driven by the spirit of whatever it takes to succeed, people's passion, goodwill, integrity, and commitment once again prevailed. But I left Switzerland with an unsettled feeling.

The *Telesis* issue correctly projected a virtual downpour of bandwidth and huge demand for powerful new digital transmission techniques, though the implications in terms of insight and the scope of the opportunity were not projected at all. It said, "Adding to this downpour are rapidly increasing mobility capabilities ushered in by the wireless revolution. To take full advantage of these changes, designers must imagine (and create) a world in which bandwidth is virtually limitless and free and where devices are untethered and can roam anywhere on the planet." These words complemented a quote of mine in Peter Newman's book in a feature on user-centered innovation. I said, "With the advent of broadband and mobility, the old rules are gone. Like the painters during the European Renaissance, telecommunication designers have been given a new medium in which to work and a powerful new set of tools."

While I said these words and tried to sell the message, I stood with others throughout the company in Ottawa, Calgary, Dallas, Harlow, and France in the belief that we needed to proactively respond to the downpour.

Organizations must adapt or die and the same applies to innovation. Too often, organizations revel in their past successes and their own rhetoric. They begin to believe the press clippings they themselves created. In my experience, every time an organization loses its way the reason is known within the company and a solution is either under way in some form or being suppressed by colliding values at the top. In the classic case of corporate failure, it is management's reveling in success combined with a refusal to listen that causes the organization to fall a critical step behind. The new Nortel was content to rest on its Northern Telecom laurels.

As a colleague succinctly put it, the company was "asleep at the switch."

It wasn't that we in BNR purple and our brethren in Nortel blue hadn't tried to move the company forward and realize an array of possible futures. But we sometimes felt like quarterbacks with no receivers downfield.

We led the market for three generations of business terminals, for example, and tasted great opportunity with Displayphone in 1983. The first integrated voice and data terminal eventually failed because it was essentially empty. It lacked a real connection and a commitment to our exploratory email system. The first terminal with a touch interface languished in our labs until, in frustration, I commissioned an elegant colour photograph complete with a fresh red rose and the product misted with water. I couriered the photograph to David Vice, then Northern's president, and to BNR president John Roth with a note saying, "Someone will make this product. The question is, who?" They tore down the barricades of resistance and the MeridianTouchphone was introduced to the world in February 1985. Later positioned as the "dashboard" of a Rolls-Royce Meridian SL-1 system, Chrysler chairman Lee Iacocca demanded the terminal for his desk as a condition of the system purchase. He got it.

But Nortel now considered the terminal—the primary user connection to the network—a secondary priority. The company abandoned the consumer division and closed its London and Nashville plants in 1994, reducing by almost half the terminal manufacturing and development capacity, leaving only Belleville for manufacturing and Mountain View and Calgary for product development. I had integrated the remnants of BNR's terminal development function into the Corporate Design Group some years earlier. When we ventured into cell phones, we were fortunate to have a partner with Matra in France, a partnership engineered years earlier by Paul Stern.

Nevertheless, even without receivers downfield and without choice, but with the passion and commitment of innovators never willing to accept defeat, we at CDG proceeded with the confidence and support of George Smyth and Brian Hewat to continue exploratory development and end-user analysis.

But to move forward requires an unyielding commitment to innovation and maintaining technology leadership. That's what had made Northern Telecom great. But by 1995, the company abandoned that position. The definition of the core business changed from "design and manufacture of telecommunications equipment" to "design, deployment, and integration of digital networks," while the stated market positioning changed from "technology leader" to "global resource for digital network solutions and services."

Continuous innovation requires an adaptive organization that can execute on its promise, recognize where the market will be, be willing to obsolete and cannibalize its own products, and leave catch-up to its competitors. The gap between product innovation and sustaining development is a cultural chasm. It's the difference between "bet the business" and "protect market share."

Telecom '95 seemed to me to mark a crucial transformation in corporate direction. The combination of the centennial and the World of Networks initiatives conveyed a heads-down position affecting Nortel's future and its leadership position. While being network-centric and recognizing the market's insatiable appetite for more bandwidth, Nortel barely acknowledged the influence of mobility, the discontinuity created by smart phones like Orbitor, or the wide open door for continued innovation. The Internet and the web were almost passing references for a corporation which years before anticipated such major discontinuities and capitalized on them. I feared that Nortel had now left itself exposed to competitors and market dynamics well beyond management's control.

9 MAKING A TURN

With the centennial behind us, 1996 ushered in yet another massive wave of change for the new Nortel, powered not only by rising market demand and global expansion, but also by an even greater emphasis on the changes to the corporation Jean Monty had outlined the year before. Over the next few months he put great effort into communicating that the old Northern Telecom was gone. Poof. The past is past, so forget it and move on.

The campaign kicked into high gear in February when Jean gave a *State of Nortel* address to the Senior Management Conference in San Francisco. Walter Light had established the tradition of holding SMCs 15 years before as the T-100, a talent management initiative originally designed to identify potential candidates for core executive management career planning and development. Over time, the number of attendees had grown to several hundred. It remained a mystery to me how I ever got there or why I continued to attend, as I don't recall ever taking part in any personal career development discussions. But the meetings became useful for delivering leaderships' views, for breakout sessions on issues of concern, and for enjoyable networking with old friends.

That year, Jean provided an overview of his stewardship since the massive write down he'd announced just after becoming CEO. He detailed what had been accomplished over the three years since, what had happened in 1995, and what the plans were for 1996. The subtitle of his address—*Facing a New Future*—was heavily influenced by the underlying trends in the industry. His address was an honest reflection of where we were at the time, network-centric to a fault.

"The strategy introduced in 1995," he said, "resulted from three years of intense efforts to restructure, redefine, and prepare the company for the realities and opportunities of an industry that is itself in the midst of an historic transformation. For both the company and the industry, these [three] years have been a fertile period of creativity, innovation, and *un virage*—a hard turn from the past. In a few years, we'll be able to look back and reflect on 1995 and see how important it was as a sharp turn to the future. Nineteen-ninety-five was a point of demarcation, the dividing line between the strategies that defined the Northern Telecom of the past 20 years and the new Nortel that is opening up to a new set of opportunities."

It wouldn't be the last hard turn for the company before the millennium.

One of the seven challenges Jean laid out for 1996 was branding and how he wanted to end the proliferation of names. We soon learned what that meant. Later in February came a day that to me should go down in infamy. Word came down that the name of our R&D organization would no longer be BNR, the proud powerhouse of innovation widely recognized around the world as an aligned but separate company. BNR's 14,000 product development employees were now absorbed directly and completely into the four lines of business. The remaining 3,000 of us working on core technology and future product design would be known as Nortel Technology, a new division of the corporation.

The changes were rationalized in corporate speak around the need "to bring all the corporation's design and development resources under the Nortel brand." Just as Northern Telecom remained the legal name of the company now known everywhere as Nortel, BNR Ltd. would legally remain for tax, trademark, and other purposes (especially R&D tax credits), but BNR as a visible symbol for the corporation would be tossed into the trashcan of history.

To many of us R&D types, the announcement was received like a dagger to the heart. To no one's surprise, I took it harder than most. Then things got worse. In an act of belligerence that touched every BNR employee, within a few months corporate logo cops descended on the Ottawa campus and over a single weekend removed every bit of evidence that BNR had ever existed. I just managed to save the brushed aluminum wall-mounted logo from our lobby (and still have it). The mighty roadway plinth marking the entrance to the main campus was shorn of its purple raiment and draped in Nortel blue. What the local children once called "The Big Purple Book" we now called a crying shame.

The very soul of the corporate vision—BNR's spirit of innovation, dedication, and excellence—was cast out by the stroke of a pen. Vision can imbed itself into the corporate culture and impact the spirit of every employee. Vision is a visceral thing. It becomes a trust that instills pride, purpose, and commitment, as the thousands of BNR alumni who claim to bleed purple blood can attest. Whether they were scientists, software designers, executives, or maintenance workers, chances are they would still say to this day, "I loved my job and I loved where I worked." That trust took a severe beating as the corporate crown jewel, the source of the lifeblood of Nortel's success vanished, chewed up, swallowed, and digested by the corporate lines of business. Disowning BNR would be a defining moment in shaping Nortel's fate.

Through the rest of the year, Monty continued pushing the message of Nortel's change from a hardware manufacturer to a digital systems designer and integrator and a global resource for the world's network builders. He put special emphasis on the shift in focus from hardware to software he said was at the heart of the company's transformation. In and of itself, this was a continuation of the networking position to market, though it also sounded to me like reveling in corporate rhetoric and success. Yet again, it failed to embrace the implications of the pending market disruption of the Internet, the web, and mobility.

I was getting more and more anxious about that disruption and discontinuity and more than a little concerned that we were at risk of moving from being an industry leader to a late follower. Frustrated, I approached Brian and George with an outrageous idea that they tentatively supported but, sensitive to certain implications, insisted I first sell to John Roth, now Nortel's president and chief operating officer, before coming out strongly in favour.

There was an Executive Council meeting coming up in Toronto and I booked a meeting during the lunch break outside the hotel conference room. There, I pitched the idea of *Share And Discover* to John and Clarence Chandran, the president of the public carrier networks business and a member of John's inner circle. *Share And Discover* would be a day set aside for an event somewhere between a science fair and a sidewalk sale. On that day, every Nortel lab in the world would be shut down to customers and other outsiders, all meetings would be cancelled, and staff would publicly demonstrate their R&D work-in-progress. The meetings would be augmented by real-time global video links and appropriate security that excluded visitors and media.

Clarence went straight to the same implications that concerned Brian and George. Did I have any idea of the lost productivity and cost of 14,000 R&D employees essentially taking a day off?

"Of course," I said, "But imagine the gain if two or three discover the advantage of similar work that can be leveraged through new collaboration. Everyone wins." They warmed to the idea and John asked if I had a budget. I replied I didn't need one because after 30 years' experience I knew that no decent manager could predict an annual budget within five percent and probably had more than that built in as contingency. I also assured him that we could cover the costs of the video links in our IT budget. Sold.

My next problem was figuring out how to get the buy-in from everybody else in the R&D community. Initial reactions were split between "Are you nuts?" and "Love it!" but, thankfully, it turned out to be a relatively easy internal sell. Then, in the long-standing spirit of our R&D culture and armed with the resources of CDG, we set out to market the event. To no one's surprise, design was front and centre, with a great iconic logo, campaign buttons, and T-shirts and posters delivered around the world. To create a little healthy competition, we used an online bulletin board that highlighted early group commitments. Creativity reigned.

The event was set for October 21, 1996. Walking the halls in Ottawa late the night before, I discovered groups setting up displays outside their labs while others moved into the building's giant atrium where we'd set up large screens for the live videoconferencing. Calls to regional labs confirmed they were all up to the same thing. Arriving early the next morning, I discovered activity everywhere from technicians testing the global links to volunteers inflating balloons. Many groups, entirely on their own initiative, had banners, team hats, and T-shirts. A Dixieland band warmed everyone up for the 11:00 am start of the global conference. We moved from lab to lab where each group introduced themselves and shared the highlights of their work.

Share and Discover was delivered on time and better than on budget, which is easier to accomplish when you don't have a budget and innovators are motivated to share. Innovators share a common attribute. When empowered with the freedom to create, they will do so at the first opportunity and in their own way.

Within the company, the event was generally considered quite a success. Privately, I was a little disappointed. With a few exceptions, most of the work shared was from sustaining product development and technology-centric components. There was very little exciting exploratory work on display. I had gone out of my way to avoid influencing the content of any presentation and shouldn't have been surprised that development labs would mostly show development. In what turned out to be more like a tradeshow than science fair, demos were predominately network-centric and heads-down. The day failed to expose the growing gap in our exploratory research investment, particularly in the Internet, wireless, and mobility. I wondered what had happened to our corporate vision: "People, reaching out to the challenge of bringing the world together, all in the spirit of leadership, innovation, dedication, and excellence."

While fully active with exciting work, a few colleagues and I were noticing disturbing changes in the corporate culture. With the dramatic shift of power and control to the global lines of business, what was left of the R&D organization was becoming an easy excuse for anything going wrong, including delays, slow to market, and rising costs. As pricing pressure increased, so did the blame. If competitors caught up or new entrants to the field such as Cisco beat us to market, R&D was at fault.

The decentralized organizations became partitioned and isolated from the mother ship, demoralizing staff at every level. Change of behaviour at the top sent clear signals to everyone below: whatever you're doing, it's just not good enough or fast enough. President John Roth, obsessed by speed on the track where he raced his classic car collection and in business where he raced the structure he had created, was clear. Speed to market, rather than new value and innovation, was the goal we were pursuing.

Charged by rapid growth and market expansion, yet impervious to several winds of change and unaware of the turmoil created within, Nortel went on a huge construction spree, building new labs, manufacturing facilities, and offices, especially in Ottawa. The region was already home to the

162

largest concentration of Nortel workers in the world, with more than 10,000 employees and plans to hire another 5,000 by the year 2000.

Nortel still took great pride in its Canadian roots. The centennial history noted that the company spent $1.6 billion on R&D in 1994 and over half of it—52 percent—was done in Canada. That year, Northern and BNR hired one out of every three Canadian Masters and PhD graduates in electrical engineering and computer science. Fifty-five Canadian high-tech companies active in 1995 owed their parentage to Nortel and BNR, numbers that continued to grow until 2000.

George, Brian, and I often met informally, sometimes all three of us, though usually just one on one. None of us could believe or understand the massive construction and recruitment drive taking place. We worried that executives were spending too much time reveling in their own press clippings and were building out in anticipation of a global market that—they hoped and prayed—had an insatiable demand for what we offered. We all thought it was nuts. What if things changed and the bubble burst?

With construction getting underway, the now not so little Corporate Design Group was forced to relocate in Ottawa while also needing new quarters in Harlow and in Calgary, our third office that focused on cellular and other wireless product development. Thanks to Brian Hewat and George Smyth, CDG was able to get two new buildings of its own and at least a new office location in Calgary.

Besides Labs 1 through 5, the Carling campus in Ottawa soon boasted Corporate Design House, the administration and executive building first used by Northern Electric to launch the company's R&D programs in the 1960s. Now totally renovated, refurbished, and upgraded to house CDG, the new design created the illusion of a village by constructing four small stand-alone corner buildings under the 30-foot open ceiling. Each had space for exhibits and demonstrations on their ground floors and private conference rooms on the second. The buildings joined by open bridges accessed via a wide spiral staircase. Never missing an opportunity to throw a party, we held a grand opening, complete with federal, provincial, and municipal politicians. Rather than going with the traditional ribbon cutting, we had over 75 of our children (we were a prolific bunch) waiting outside the auditorium's two side entrances. On cue—the words "Welcome to Corporate Design House"—they burst through the doors cheering, ran up the centre aisle, and exited through the rear door. The kids were rewarded with pizza and T-shirts while we had lunch and conducted tours.

In contrast, the Harlow building was the smallest on its campus. Built during the Cold War for radar research (in the service of British counter-intelligence, so it was rumoured), it featured a small ground floor lab and an isolated windowless test room on top that we converted to a conference room. In keeping with the smallest building theme, we created a mini-grand opening, sent out mini invitations, and rented four Austin Minis to chauffeur our guests to the front door to be welcomed by campus staff. It was quite a sight watching them trying to get out of the back seats of the Minis to join us for tours and a catered lunch that featured mini-bite-sized sandwiches. Thank God all the guests of honour were good-natured.

With **R&D** funds under **LOB** control, the four lines of business went on hiring sprees in anticipation of future market demands, assuming that if we built the customer, base profits would rise. We even got to the point of financing our customers' debt. A former senior manager in corporate design who left to become a director in HR confided that the company had more than 500 recruiters—100 in Canada, 400 in the U.S.—with a mandate to hire 7,000 people. Current employees were offered cash incentives (bounties) for referring potential candidates. I recall job fairs feeling like carnivals as prospective employees arrived by the busload.

Change was everywhere as 1996 wound down. Brian Hewat retired and wasn't replaced, George Smyth, BNR's last president, relocated to the U.S. to head the AT&T account, and John Roth named Gedas Sakus president of Nortel Technology. Gedas was a former president of both Northern Telecom Canada and the public carrier networks organization, and was a very long-term employee (his was the first desk moved into Northern Electric's Bramalea switching plant in 1962). A first-class operations executive, a fine coach, and a gentleman of high ethical standards, he was a joy to work with. Welcomed by everyone, he didn't relocate to Ottawa, maintaining his office at corporate headquarters in Brampton outside Toronto, and commuting to our lab complex in what by then was called Silicon Valley North. The choice may have been yet another sign of things to come.

Gedas was optimistic by nature. He was people-centric and company loyal. He disliked conflict and worked to ensure continuity across the perennial tribal instincts of product development teams in the lines of business. Hindered by a multiplicity of direct and dotted-line reporting relationships, he was forced to manage by annual and quarterly cabinet reviews before a Futures Council (a descriptor which always sounded like an oxymoron to me). Initially chaired by Brian Hewat and then by John Roth, the Futures Council always met at the Toronto Airport Sheraton Hotel for John's convenience. Productive in the beginning, I felt the tone changed as John became impatient and increasingly sounded more like a chief technology officer than a president or COO.

Our chief information officer at Nortel Technology, for example, believed that the company was seriously underestimating the profound impact of the Internet and the web on our business. He brought the issue to the attention of the senior management of the organization (what used to be called the BNR cabinet). Suitably impressed by his very detailed presentation, we placed it on the agenda of the next

Futures Council meeting. There, he presented an urgent appeal to address both the implications and the opportunities involved. His presentation was ceremoniously dismissed and discounted as the discussion was deflected toward other issues. His input resulted only in defining an action item for the non-R&D marketing executive guests of the Council who were asked to come back to the next meeting with an analysis of Nortel's position vis-à-vis Cisco Systems. As I recall, the review said we were well placed to handle any threat from Cisco. The Futures Council, to no one's surprise, soon met less frequently.

Back to work, and with the full support of the new president of wireless, CDG's Ottawa and Calgary labs continued engaging with Matra in France and their AEG subsidiary in Germany to refine the industrial design and the user interface and user experience for the evolving wireless handset portfolio. Matra's radio technology had been critical to our prototype demo of Orbitor at Telecom '95.

BellSouth was the lead customer for our first cellular handset, featuring better acoustics and launched for the North American market in September 1996. It was reputed to be the first cellphone that displayed the name of the caller, using the phone system's local name and number directory.

We launched the next version of the Nortel/Matra cellphone, featuring a personal speakerphone and voice-activated dialing, at CeBit, held annually in March in Hanover, Germany. CeBit was the world's biggest IT event spanning the computing and communications industries, albeit without the glamour of similar events in Las Vegas and New York. In the wrap-up to CeBit '97, *The Cellphone Magazine* featured our cellphone on the cover and later that year gave it the magazine's annual award of excellence.

Besides new physical quarters, the summer of 1997 also brought yet more changes to our R&D organization. Nortel Technology, the organization that replaced BNR a year earlier, was officially dismantled. In a directive that, in the first instance, seemed somewhat comical, president and COO

John Roth announced "an important change" involving Gedas Sakus's responsibilities and title. "Gedas' title will change from President, Nortel Technology, to President, Technology, Nortel." Naturally, many more important details followed. The change was apparently made to eliminate confusion among customers, the media, and employees who thought of Nortel Technology as separate from Nortel—in other words, a BNR in all but name—even though it was only a division within the company.

Gedas still had direct responsibility for advanced technology, which included work by my corporate design team, physical design, core systems engineering, and the supply and components group. But with the new edict, we were no longer Nortel Technology employees. Thereafter, we would be referred to as the Advanced Technology Group, with a focus on core technologies and future designs. All it meant to me was printing yet another new business card.

We were fully active with exciting developments, with the majority of our people engaged in leading edge technologies. We worked with Sun Microsystems' Java technology as the platform for Orbitor and Vista and created little programs that could be provisioned and brokered by wireless service providers and be downloaded to the handset. We called them applets then, known today as apps. We unwittingly became part of the open-versus-proprietary battle then being waged between Sun's Scott McNealy on the Java side, and Bill Gates in the Windows corner. In what became a love-in at his JavaOne conference, McNealy praised Nortel's vision of the future.

New Magellan products for transmission were still coming online. There was exploratory work on network management and service deployment systems. The Proximity fixed wireless access products, which used digital radio rather than copper cable to link businesses and residences to the public telephone network, and continued to reduce the time and cost of network construction and deployment, especially in developing countries. By the late nineties, Proximity networks were in service or under construction in dozens of countries in Europe, Asia, and North, Central, and South America.

We worked with the University of Ottawa Heart Institute to evaluate a telehealth system to improve access to cardiac consultations and specialized health services in remote areas of Ontario, using what would in later years be called tablets to conduct physical examinations by video and electronic stethoscopes. Work with Ottawa hospitals involved maintaining patient records as well as remote diagnostics.

For SoundBeam, our innovative approach to wearable audio, we moved forward to prototype development and field trials. As always, we took user value as our lodestar. We had evaluated listening devices such as corded and cordless headsets, cordless phones, speakerphones, and single-ear earphones earlier in the decade. We had worked with businesses and other user groups to determine the specific design attributes that could deliver audio privacy, audio quality, comfort, and image. The result was the SoundBeam Neckset for use in hands-free telephony and desktop communications.

What some said looked like a question mark hung around the neck, provided the user with hands-free operation, privacy, and mobility by having two technically amazing directional speakers mounted on the user's shoulders and a directional microphone placed on the chest. A button could activate speech recognition features or deactivate it in noisy environments. Trial users were sometimes taken aback by its high-tech look, but loved it when they actually put it on and often reported forgetting to take it off. In 1998, MIT's Media Lab adapted SoundBeam principles in developing its own nomadic audio environment platform.

There were new developments and tremendous churn evident everywhere as continuous change ran rampant throughout the industry. The market was growing at a rapid rate and also consolidating, exemplified by the purchase of MCI by WorldCom in 1997 for $37 billion, then one of the largest mergers in American history. It made WorldCom, for a time, the second largest long-distance phone company after AT&T, with the two obviously at war for new customers. Nortel jumped at the opportunity to be an arms-supplier to both sides.

For me, continuous change started with additional accountability. My title now read "Vice-president, Corporate Design Group + Physical Design and Technology (PDT)." PDT was a very large group of more than 500 employees, with offices in Ottawa, Harlow, and throughout the U.S. It focused on sustained hardware development and outsourcing manufacturing to companies such as Celestica and Flextronics. It was also accountable for implementing Y2K initiatives and ISO-9000, the international quality management system. PDT managed the programs through scheduled audits and quarterly reports, a process which proved difficult for me. I didn't—and still don't—think innovation, process, and content guys are a good mix. They can drive each other nuts. But I accepted the responsibility and did the best I could.

For Nortel, continuous change became visible in new growth and a new CEO. Jean Monty and John Roth had been a good team in the short run, managing an impressive turnaround. Revenues that hit a $10 billion milestone in 1995 increased to almost $13 billion in 1996 and more than $15 billion in 1997. Jean was named Canadian CEO of the year in 1997 and promptly returned as CEO to BCE, the parent company of both Nortel and Bell. There he was determined to make Bell the service supplier of choice in the Internet revolution, eventually leading Bell on an acquisition spree into e-commerce. To no one's surprise, John Roth took up the reins as Nortel's new CEO in October 1997.

There were other changes of personnel in the offing. Colin Beaumont had retired as chief engineer of BNR at the end of 1995 and hadn't been replaced. David Twyver, president of the wireless networks business and a champion of our work, now quit to become CEO of Craig McCaw's Teledesic, a commercial broadband satellite constellation based in Seattle. Lower levels of the organization seemed impervious to the changes, but I was feeling the loss of longstanding coaches and friends. They had been lots of fun to work with and had been complementary to my values, skill set, and eccentric personality. I was feeling a distinct loss of personal influence.

Roth's appointment as CEO of Nortel was initially well received. He had been a familiar presence for decades. In my case, I arrived at Northern Electric's new Ottawa labs in 1966 and John in 1969 via the satellite business in which Northern was then still involved. Our careers diverged early. While I discovered my passion for innovation and R&D, John, an engineer and product guy, took the path of operations management, rotating quickly through the ranks of the Northern development stream and becoming a first-class operations executive. I first worked with him transferring new product R&D to manufacturing. As a plant general manager, he was decisive, willing to delegate, and a firm believer in cost avoidance before production in contrast to the long-standing tradition of cost reduction after the fact. I later worked with him on the associated market development programs of OPEN World, FiberWorld, and A World of Networks. He was an important leader in driving continuity across the product platforms and their future.

I always liked him. Self-confident and soft-spoken, with an infectious laugh, he was contemplative and a good listener. John was a private person and first and foremost a family guy. He wasn't one to engage in much casual social conversation or idle chatter and his meetings were always effective and efficient. He seemed energized in town hall meetings, being best in class in that setting.

I preferred face-to-face meetings and, over the years, he was always available, always supportive of my initiatives, and always decisive. We always got along well, though I would not have called him a champion, let alone a patron, of my enthusiasms. I never felt any close kinship. To me, he was always something of an enigma. While giving him due credit for being a top-notch operations executive, I never considered him a visionary, especially compared to Robert Scrivener, Don Chisholm, or Walter Light. It was his greatest weakness. But, given his early R&D experience, I felt he had empathy for new product innovation and was delighted when he was appointed president of BNR, which he ran well. He was a good boss, effective, efficient, and smart.

He was usually considered an internal product guy with BNR blood, but that perception changed somewhat with his decentralization of R&D and the creation of the four global profit-centered lines of business. To me, R&D was—and is— collaborative and dependent on the leadership of a very small group of kindred spirits. Operating like a sub-culture, membership is by undeclared invitation only. The members will maintain a project through faith and drive the pinstripes nuts by rarely, if ever, meeting and by never documenting the discussion when they do. I can't suggest that John had any desire to be part of the sub-culture or saw the need for collaboration. He never seemed to be a kindred spirit of what became known as the purple brotherhood, which perhaps may be interpreted as a diplomatic way of saying he alienated a lot of his former colleagues and wasn't always trusted.

Perceptions also changed when, soon after taking office, he created an acquisition task force and then, in December 1997, issued his renowned right-angle turn and webtone declaration to all employees. In it, he noted that data traffic on backbone networks had exceeded the volume of voice traffic in 1996 and that all communications was migrating from telephone networks to networks based on the Internet Protocol (IP). He set Nortel's new task as building webtone networks that could carry Internet and data traffic with the same kind of reliability, integrity, security, and capacity that we all took for granted in the familiar world of dialtone. He said everyone had to get up to speed and become more expert about what IP networking could do.

A couple of months later, on March 2, 1998, he again sent to all employees a six-page memo titled "Developing a 'Right-Angle' Culture." In it, he opined: "In my December memo to all employees, I talked about the need for Nortel to make what I call a 'right-angle turn'—to become a company that thinks about data and IP networking first and about voice second rather than the other way around. In that memo, I laid out three key challenges. I challenged us to work together: to make Nortel a recognized leader in, and perhaps even THE creator of, webtone networks; to master the business of our data networking competitors before they become as good as we are at building rugged and reliable networks; to become more literate and knowledgeable than our competitors and our customers about the Internet, TCP/IP, and the World Wide Web."

The letter continued with a treatise on speed to market—short development cycles and short times to market, described as short/short. Ironically, he also said, "If we miss the window of opportunity, it's an opportunity lost forever." He was right.

His quarterly letters to all employees were a carryover from his days as COO and were generally well received. But to me, the tone had changed. The new tone reflected frustration and clearly communicated a breakdown of trust between R&D and the CEO. He thought R&D had become too large and too slow. The R&D community was not without blame. Notwithstanding our attempts to address Nortel's exposure to the market dynamics created by the Internet with exploratory product, the R&D machine had become consumed by the iterative process of incremental product development. John was right that our development cycles were too long and we were too slow in multi-sourcing components and outsourcing manufacture. Cisco had already become the industry's best-in-class reference for outsourcing manufacturing.

The change in tone signaled to me that he had made up his mind and had stopped listening to anyone associated with our success to date. Turning his back on a history of global success brought about by internal R&D investments, he decided that his only option was to buy time and market share through acquisitions and enlisting new leadership from outside the corporation.

From a culture that took pride in its inclusive manner of management, executive power became exclusive to the concentrated few. When Roth left BNR and returned to Northern in the late 1980s, Frank Dunn had become his most trusted sidekick and they moved up the ranks in tandem, John in operations and Frank in finance. As he moved through the positions of president, COO, and CEO, he assembled a small core group of wise insiders such as Dunn, Art McDonald, Clarence Chandran, Gedas Sakus, and Jim Long whose counsel he seemed to seek and listen to, though sometimes he seemed to operate as a lone wolf.

Many of us who were a touch skeptical about the new direction wondered whether there had been any challenge by the board of directors or by non-executive chairman Frank Carlucci or later Lynton (Red) Wilson as John negotiated and ratified the single largest strategic redirection of the business since the creation of BNR in 1972.

Buoyed by rapid growth, the board seemed impervious to the implications of the redirection. Concentrated power at the top was too isolated from an alternate future known within the rest of the organization. Lulled by success, the focus of both the board and the executive soon shifted to the addictive attraction of rising share prices, stock options, market capitalization, and industry adulation. Unfortunately, such metrics, along with success and wealth, are trailing indicators. They reflect futures past. They breed complacent behaviour. Inept and out of touch, the board members either couldn't challenge John or simply chose not to. In the first few months of 1998, the Nortel behemoth ingested Broadband Networks, Aptis Communications, and Cambrian Systems, the first morsels in a $20 billion acquisition spree that defined the next few years.

Discouraged, yet undaunted, many of us continued with the zeal and passion of evangelists to convince the company that the real opportunity of webtone lay outside the comfort zone of our network-centric view. Building on the Orbitor concept and the success of our Vista smart edge-of-network line of terminals, I renamed the R&D terminals team—at their suggestion—Network Edge Technology (NET). We built a presentation centre to be featured as part of the customer tours in Ottawa. The network-edge vision was a strategic move to draw paradoxical attention to the entrenched view inside Nortel that the network was the centre of the communications world. That view dovetailed nicely with the networking position to market I created in Nashville, but that had been ten years before. The world had changed dramatically. I said at the time, "Paradoxically, the centre has moved to the edge and the end user is now the new centre of the network."

Sometime in the early winter of 1998, I was appointed VP for advanced technology and strategic planning, with four assistant VP groups and an operating budget a touch over $50 million. I took advantage of the new position to change CDG's name back to Design Interpretive. While I still had responsibility for corporate design and physical design technology, I also gained responsibility for developing our strategic plan and for our Montreal lab founded as BNR Nun's Island during the Chisholm era.

The Nun's Island lab, co-located with the Institut National de la Recherche Scientifique, had become regarded as a world-class center in speech recognition and systems engineering on par with Bell Labs, Carnegie Mellon University, and IBM. The advanced research delivered world-class algorithms and a slew of intellectual properties. Its applied research was successfully deployed in telcos for automated billing and directory assistance and in automotive speech and voice recognition for hands-free phones. In the mid- to late-nineties, the lab's collaborative work with the network-edge technology group in Ottawa was integral to the development of Orbitor and the first applications to VoIP terminals.

The staff was terrific, with a great sense of pride, and I enjoyed working with them. They loved to recall with much affection a young research engineer in computer systems, natural language processing, and automatic speech recognition who had worked at Nun's Island in 1992. The brilliant Julie Payette went directly from BNR to NASA, becoming a well-travelled astronaut and the first Canadian to set foot on the International Space Station.

As far as strategic planning was concerned, my job, using my small strategic planning staff, was to pull the plan together and orchestrate bilateral meetings with R&D people in the lines of business. The advanced technology program was to be managed by a small board, accountable to Gedas Sakus, set up to manage the rationalized product development matrix. But with 90 percent of the R&D budget controlled by the lines of business, the $180 million-plus advanced technology program had no one accountable for the strategy or for tracking its effectiveness. Nobody actually owned the right-angle turn to webtone or was accountable for actually executing the turn. Confusing to many, the board was just another committee supported by corporate rhetoric.

But I accepted the webtone declaration with some optimism and went to great effort to embrace the webtone challenge almost exclusively and obsequiously in the three-year *Strategic Plan: 1999-2001*, which I presented to John's executive council in April 1998.

Along with key product developments, alliances, investments, and moves to promote greater agility over the coming years, the presentation laid out various plans to get everyone up to speed on IP, including a *Webtone Technology Day* to focus on web applications, a *Webtone Flight School* to explore necessary cultural shifts, and *Share and Discover 2* based on the theme "I Speak IP." John endorsed that idea enthusiastically and moved his CEO Forum (the successor to the annual senior management conferences) to Ottawa to match the date in early autumn. Armed with our previous experience and success, we created a new campaign and a website on our own access-secured intranet.

I looked forward optimistically to a stimulating and exciting spring, but two events in the next couple of months radically altered my outlook. The first was a corporate decision about the forward-looking products we'd been developing for almost a decade. We were still the only company developing a Java-enabled smart phone with a touch-sensitive graphical user interface and a client-server way to download apps from the network. We had an internal trial period near the validation phase of Orbitor's design, and I took great delight in seeing employee test subjects working out the system's bugs as they wandered through the labs editing emails and sending messages to colleagues.

We demonstrated the first working prototypes of Orbitor at the GSM World Congress in Cannes in early 1998, which attracted some attention from the high-tech media for the device's potential as a market-leading innovation and game-changing product for the industry. We manufactured 80 finished units for market and service delivery trials set to begin in Europe a few months later with Britain's BT Cellnet, one of Europe's largest cell phone operators, which had come on as a lead customer in 1997.

Meanwhile, in March 1998, in other handset developments, we introduced the first manufactured product based on adapted Orbitor concepts and principles at CeBit '98. Named Europa, the cellular phone included the touch sensitive screen, the slide down keyboard, a directory, and a note pad and quick notes. Introduced to the market first in Europe, it was later sold and distributed by Fido and Bell in Canada.

After the success with Europa at CeBIT and while readying Orbitor for field trials, Nortel decided to get out of the cellular terminal business altogether. It was a decision that shocked many and appalled more than a few. We may have convinced John that the opportunity was too big. We couldn't be first in all industry segments or be all things to all men. Management was clearly unwilling to compete with the market momentum then led by Nokia, Ericsson, and Motorola.

In John's view, Nortel's design skills were concentrated in the heavy-duty technology at the core of large systems rather than consumer products. (He was quoted in one publication as saying Nortel had little experience with consumer products, or perhaps misquoted since that's what the company had been producing for more than a hundred years.) He just didn't think Nortel could design and manufacture mobile units quickly enough or cheaply enough to compete on a cost-competitive basis with industry leaders.

It's true that we were used to designing products that had a life expectancy of five or ten years or more. With Orbitor, we would have to create new models every year or 18 months or so. You can do wonders with temporary tools to create prototypes for customer trials, but getting the corporate commitment to invest tens of millions of dollars in high-volume manufacturing is always another story.

Development of the Vista Javaphone that allowed apps to be downloaded from the network was soon cancelled. The members of Orbitor's development team scattered. Don Lindsay, the head of the team designing the user interface, left to take up a position with Apple before moving on to Microsoft and RIM. Almost ten years later, Apple's iPhone borrowed heavily from Orbitor's design values. Ahead of their time, the technology and intellectual property we developed would later be overtaken and delivered by the Internet, the web, and the soon-to-be-ubiquitous browser.

Left with only a large array of patent filings and no outlet for continuous innovation, we redeployed our resources to focus on speech recognition technologies, wireless local area networks, and fixed wireless access networks.

The decision marked the end of the network-edge vision. Private enterprise is not a democracy. The top of the house owns the right to be wrong. We foresaw the opportunity to once again spearhead a fundamental paradigm shift in telecommunications as we had done several times before. We had all the talent, the means, and the opportunity to do so. We let it pass.

Most of Nortel was content and secure in its future, buoyed by record sales and massive expansion, albeit without any metric to measure future vulnerability. To the chagrin of the few of us who reached out to where the market would be and had defined an exciting alternate future based on the wide open world of personal mobility, the right-angle turn and webtone vision would be implemented within our network-centric tradition and ultimately lead to a dead end. I recall doodling a cartoon in my lab book based on one of my favourite Yogi Berra quotes, "If you come to a fork in the road, take it."

The second event that changed my outlook was the bombshell announcement on June 15, 1998, just weeks before *Share and Discover 2*, that Nortel would buy Cisco's main competitor, Bay Networks, for $9.1 billion dollars and appoint David House, Bay's CEO, president of Nortel. The acquisition brought in more than 7,000 new employees with specialized knowledge of sending voice, video, and data over the Internet.

In a world where most large acquisitions fail, analysts often cite the Not Invented Here (NIH) syndrome, industry jargon for resistance to change: head-in-the sand, out of-touch, and professionally belligerent. Easy to say and hard to prove, it's a form of condemnation and an insult to applied research scientists. I saw no evidence of it in our case. Once we in R&D got over the shock, most of us took the leap of faith and tried to get on with the job. Analysts also often cite a collision of cultures as a reason for failure, and I'd say that in our case speed to market, interval to market, and telecom versus data did pose some problems.

John's memo to employees in June 1998 identified local area networks (LAN) and wide area networks (WAN) as the new frontier for communications. "Being the first to deliver these new generation networks to customers is a big growth opportunity. I see [the Bay acquisition] as an investment in the future of the company and the major step in making the 'right-angle turn' Nortel needed to achieve our webtone vision."

Following the announcement in mid-June, John and David House soon set off to travel the world for a series of employee town hall meetings designed to stabilize the organization, excite employees with the fervently imagined opportunity, and appeal for their commitment during the transition. The tour was the right thing to do and was well received. I overheard at a town hall meeting, "They look like Batman and Robin."

I met House no more than twice and never personally beyond a formal greeting. He didn't stay around long, so I can only assume he came with a set of golden handcuffs, industry jargon for a system of financial incentives to keep an employee from leaving the company for a minimum period of time, an arrangement typical for CEOs in major mergers and acquisitions. House had the title; Roth had the power and control.

He was in Ottawa for John's Forum and the *Share and Discover* experience. Arriving at the conference, I was somewhat stunned by its size and the mix of attendees. There was a distinct reduction in the ratio of R&D product people to pinstripes, with executives from human resources, financial, legal, and administration the overwhelming majority. The proceedings were not as much fun as such meetings used to be. Walter's SMCs established a tradition of interaction and even Socratic debate. But John, world trade president Jim Long, and new president David House dominated this conference.

Interaction was minimal, though things started well. The first presentations and discussion in the interactive forum demonstrated the enthusiasm of a company undergoing massive expansion through acquisitions and the confidence that the world had an insatiable demand for our product, which was all well and good. As the conference progressed, however, the tone changed dramatically when some questions were seen as challenging the corporate direction. Questions were discounted and answers seemed more like directives. The implicit message was, get on the train or be left at the station. It was an example of management by fiat, with the leadership saying, "When I want your opinion, I'll give it to you."

Feeling increasingly out of touch, I slipped out, returned to the labs, and prepared to greet everyone at *Share and Discover* 2. When the global senior management team arrived, I donned my traditional campaign shirt and propeller beanie and introduced John to the employee audience in the atrium. During his opening remarks, he assigned me a new merit badge—Master of Mischief—then introduced the various research teams from around the world. Post-event analysis revealed there were 32 development labs involved, 300 live events, 150 websites getting 1.7 million hits leading up to the event, and more than 106,000 password-restricted pages downloaded.

Once again, I was disappointed with the content of the presentations. Development driven, the event still presented a network-centric telecom and carrier view, focused largely on carrying IP versus what could be done with it or the implications. There were a couple of exceptions, including the enterprise networks group that, despite being shut down and facing redeployment to other fields, showed exploratory work on IP terminals, VoIP, and the network-provisioned applets. Their presentation was one of the most memorable for me.

The other memorable demo was from my own corporate design group. Once again, I had deliberately stayed out of the group's planning. I had no idea what they were up to and they managed to keep quiet about it right up to the show. In the end, I was very impressed.

Using Orbitor and SoundBeam concepts, they created a live fashion show of wearable mobility products, performed first in the auditorium, with the show broadcast to other sites, and later throughout the crowd-filled atrium with staff dressed as emergency workers (police, fire, ambulance), health professionals (doctors and nurses), a bike-messenger, even a token pinstripe. Their work may have been cancelled but their pride and passion prevailed. Come hell or high water, they were going to show and share what marvels they had created with their colleagues throughout Nortel's global empire. Good for them.

The acquisitions continued into 1999 and 2000, with now-forgotten corporate names such as Clarify, Promontory, and optical networking firms such as Qtera, Xros, and CoreTek being added to the mix. Some of them had no revenues or products ready for market but did have lots of employees who were unfamiliar with our business and whose core technologies rarely delivered on their promise.

The employees remaining in advanced technology were left to deal with the implications of Bay Networks and of what would become a $20-billion-dollar acquisition binge. But there were fewer and fewer interactions and discussions across the company with the new research employees from the acquisitions since almost every senior R&D executive I knew had taken early retirement or otherwise left the company. Nortel was brain dead.

After the merger with Bay Networks, I was tasked to lead Nortel's R&D organization "into the 21st century and set new strategic directions in partnership with Nortel's line of business partners." I had a committee to help, though I don't recall it ever meeting, perhaps because I wasn't the chairman or someone forgot to invite me. To me, the handwriting on the wall was clear and easily read. Personally, I had no illusions of career accomplishment. I increasingly felt like the last champion standing.

The company was still making progress, though it seemed to some of us to be illusory. Revenues were still growing, hitting almost $18 billion in 1998 and jumping to more than $22 billion in 1999. But the markets began to send a pretty clear message in late 1998 that the explosive growth the company had gotten used to would be settling down to more realistic levels. In truth, many in the company looked at the 20, 30, or 40 percent or more year-over-year growth numbers (triple-digit growth in one segment) and quietly said, "This can't go on forever." But few publicly acknowledged the adage that something that can't go on forever won't.

Gedas maintained cross-portfolio R&D continuity with regular reviews, managing consensus through a consolidated strategic plan. As VP of advanced technology strategy, I was armed with a small team of dedicated and excellent people whose advocacy for investment in advanced technology—the life-blood of innovation and the primary source of our intellectual property—continued in full force though we often felt we were fighting a losing battle.

Gedas was loyal to the R&D community and he maintained the long-standing tradition of annual patent awards started decades earlier by Don Chisholm soon after BNR was created. Given the sheer increase of patents granted, the celebration over time expanded to include inventors around the world and their partners. Gedas and his wife, Dana, were perfect hosts, and Yolanda and I had the pleasure of joining them at such events at Hilton Head, North Carolina, Mont Tremblant, Quebec, and Royal Ascot in the U.K.

I will always cherish the memory of shopping the couturiers of London for a hat suitable for the world-renowned Ladies Day at Royal Ascot in June 1998. Laughing through what seemed like a dozen shops, we eventually found the perfect chapeau for Yolanda at Debenhams on Oxford Street. Arriving at the chartered coaches to take us to Ascot the next day, it was apparent the other guys, including Gedas, had enjoyed the same experience. Everyone loves a celebration. Thanks to the organization provided by the denizens of the Harlow labs, we enjoyed a catered lunch in a private pavilion next to the track and VIP passes to the paddock area. Fabulous hats were everywhere. The inventors and their partners experienced a memorable thank you. They deserved it. They really were our strength.

Over the next few months, we in the advanced technology program began to experience what was known in corporate-speak as right sizing and de-layering, all in the interests of efficiency. There were offers to senior managers to take early retirement or accept generous severance packages. I was forced to release three of my four assistant-VP direct reports while the fourth, accountable for Y2K and ISO 9000 initiatives, was saved. Fortunately for me and for Nortel, all three were excellent managers who had succession plans in place. My own stress was alleviated somewhat by the fact that the responses of those I couldn't save were almost expressions of relief.

The next wave of change crashed in near the end of the year. As part of our regular R&D operations review process, Gedas called a meeting in Harlow for early November 1998. Given the distance and difference in time zones, many of us R&D executives left our labs around the world two or three days early to take care of additional business while in the U.K.

On the Monday morning of the review, we all awoke very early to a light flashing on our phones and a voice message from Gedas that the meeting was cancelled. He went on to say that he would be retiring effective January 1999, but, given accrued holidays, would be leaving the company on November 11th, just days away. The bombshell came when he informed us that John Roth would not replace him nor create a comparable chief technology officer position. He asked us to keep the news confidential until the next Monday when a formal announcement would be made. It must have been the most difficult call Gedas ever made. It was a lousy day for everyone. I wrote in my notebook, "We lost the war... and they are fighting for the spoils." Disheartened, we all booked early flights home.

During this period of so many executive early retirements, going-away parties, lavish or otherwise, were frowned upon as they were thought to send the wrong message. Ignoring the message, a group of us quietly decided that Gedas deserved better. Applying once again the rule about forgiveness being easier to get than permission, Yolanda and I organized a late afternoon catered event at our home. Without revealing the location, Gedas and Dana were picked up at their Ottawa hotel and delivered to the waiting guests, some of whom were old colleagues who had quietly slipped into the city. Celebration was in order. We delivered and had a great time doing it.

As 1999 loomed, I felt my world changing very much for the worse. It wasn't fun to go to work in the morning and I couldn't wait to go home at the end of the day. With my boys in high school and my daughter now old enough to really experience an adventure, Yolanda and I pulled the kids out of school before Christmas 1998 and went on a one-month tour of South Africa that included a safari and a visit with Yolanda's younger brother and his family over Christmas and New Years. While enjoying a family picnic and watching a sunset over Table Mountain in Cape Town, we discussed for the first time the idea of a millennium date for my retirement. It made sense. Accordingly, 1999 became my year of transition.

Returning home, my task was clear over the next few months: find homes for all the groups and divisions under my stewardship. I had no power or control to direct dollars or resources. I felt as if I was under the instruction, "Will the last one to leave please turn out the lights and return the key to security." I focused on finding foster homes for each of the advanced technology groups, each with its own unique core competency. I spent many after-hours days meeting with friends and colleagues, functioning more like a chaplain than an R&D executive.

Counter to my philosophical belief that even under duress an adaptive organization will continue to follow its leadership as an act of survival, I discovered that wasn't true near the top. Everyone has a "fuck-it" line and they cross it when they've had enough. I discovered mine during a conversation with a friend pondering resignation. I heard myself say, "Don't quit. Make them come to you with an offer." I realized I was talking to myself and that I too had reached the line. More revealing was that I had even lost my dark sense of humour.

A short time later, I received an early evening call from John Roth. He told me that after several discussions with various executives, he couldn't find anyone willing to accept Design Interpretive within a line of business. All the LOB presidents apparently viewed design not as a core competency worthy of investment but as a service that was just one more expense that could impact their bottom line. After so many years fighting the battle, I was back at square one, facing the same problem I had started with. Sensing the awkwardness of the conversation, I suggested a face-saving solution that John found acceptable, one that involved an ironic twist. After almost four decades with the company, I finally ended up reporting directly to the president and CEO.

The arrangement was brief. Once satisfied that foster homes had been found for the advanced technology program staff and ignoring my own advice to wait for an offer, I called John with my decision to retire. I sent out a notice on June 5, 2000 saying, "The time has come to talk of reflection, renewal, and, yes, retirement." Content with good old-fashioned conversation with friends, I quietly cleaned out my office, keeping very little, and prepared my new home office to be stocked with my old office furniture, bought from corporate assets at a large surplus discount. The bastards made me pay for delivery.

I couldn't help noticing a curious symmetry to the way things unfolded for me. I had joined the company a few years before the birth of BNR and left a couple of years after its death. I had begun my journey at Northern Electric two years after Bell acquired 100 percent of its shares. By sheer coincidence, I ended my journey at Nortel Networks a month after Bell divested the last of its shares in the company. Putting an end to long historical relationships seemed to be in vogue.

Thirty-five years from the day I started, I returned to the labs for the last time. Picked up from home by a stretch limo, my family and I went to an open house celebration on the main campus at the now re-named Design Interpretive House. Everything old was new again. Called a send off—retirement parties, as noted, being discouraged at the time—it turned into a hilarious event filled with personal stories, gag gifts, and warm reflection. Most heartening, Don Chisholm and other old friends and colleagues were there. As the day progressed, we all adjourned to my home where the celebration lasted late into the evening and, for some, into the wee hours of the morning.

A week later, snail mail delivered my retirement documents for verification and signature. While confirming the years of service dates, I noticed my job title was given as "Vice-President, Design, Discovery and Imagination."

This was quite a surprise. I had acquired many titles over the years and had produced many novel business cards to be used on appropriate occasions. When John Roth referred to me at *Share and Discover 2* as "Master of Mischief," for example, I produced a new card and, after hosting a delightful visit from the joint technology committee of Britain's House of Commons and House of Lords, received a thank-you letter in an envelope addressed to "Mr. John F. Tyson, VP, Master of Mischief, etc." I framed it to hang on my office wall.

I had granted myself the 'design, discovery and imagination' title at a time when I felt a strong need to have a little fun and, naturally, had had some business cards printed for very limited use. I recalled that the last occasion I had used one was while hosting a visit by the Royal Swedish Academy of Sciences.

After escorting King Carl Gustaf XVI through the labs, at a private luncheon in the boardroom he asked about my background. Discovering that I was an industrial designer, he told me his son was studying at the Rhode Island School of Design. He looked at my regular card, which then read vice-president, advanced technology strategy, and asked how I got my current job. Unable to resist the opportunity, I handed him my other card. When he saw vice-president, design, discovery and imagination, he smiled and said, "I think you may have the best job in Nortel. May I please have another card to send to my son?"

I have no idea how the title found its way to corporate HR and into my retirement package, but it seemed fitting that it was there as a final act of mischief. I felt that, for so many years, I did in fact have the best job in Nortel and that somehow at the end I had had the last laugh. I won!

10 LOOKING BACK

Following my retirement, I joined the ranks of observers hoping that the problems multiplying for the recently renamed Nortel Networks could be overcome. The signs of a slowdown in customer spending had become more prominent and more urgent as the millennium approached and John Roth signaled that he too would retire in the fall of 2000.

Unfortunately, his chosen successor, chief operating officer Clarence Chandran, also retired as he had been stabbed during a robbery in Singapore in 1999 and had been on extended sick leave due to several complications. It may have been just as well since some thought Clarence lacked the ruthlessness required to try to save Nortel from what seemed almost certain disaster. The board appointed Frank Dunn as CEO to manage the company as it sailed on through what can only be described as a perfect storm of rapid expansion, a tech bubble, industry consolidation, and the global collapse of customer capital investment.

The appointment didn't give me much confidence in the company's future. For an organization whose global success had been based on product and technological innovation, promoting an internal career finance executive to chief executive officer created a relationship between the board and CEO that amounted to the blind leading the blind. Neither understood product content. Both were now dependent on strategic product direction driven by R&D

executives who came from acquisitions and did not always grasp the scope and direction of Nortel's business.

It often seemed to me over the years that board members were little more than well-meaning, part-time sophisticated contractors who were well compensated to meet minimal legal requirements. During the late 1990s, the board appeared to me to be well past its best-before date. Its relationship with the executive was only ever as good as the normal structured tensions and reciprocal challenges best described as when a CEO and CFO present their strategic plan in a cold sweat and leave with new and profound respect for the board members. Without challenge, the interdependencies became too cozy, based more on ritual than value. Soft from success, the board was content to follow.

But when a board abdicates its fundamental responsibility to proactively set the strategic direction of the company and allows itself to become too remote from the corporate culture, shielded by executives who consider the directors a necessary evil, ineffective caretakers are the inevitable result. In spite of best intentions, the Nortel board, whether competent or mediocre, was isolated at the top. The only role they could play was engaging in reactive interventions during corporate crises which, as the new century unfolded, soon included class action lawsuits and questionable accounting procedures. The board of caretakers was helpless.

More smug than self-confident, both the board and the executive were prone to describing success in terms of "I did it, I deserve it." They discounted the trust and faith granted by the committed employees who created the innovations that produced the company's success. Worse yet, they lost the ability to listen. Reeling from continuous internal churn and the structural problems associated with an extremely complex restructuring, the board lost control. They fiddled while the business burned. It was a sad indictment of a board and an executive that once had the vision and courage to take on the world of communications and create a world-class corporation built on the power of innovation.

The explosive growth of the 1990s came to a screeching halt when the tech bubble burst in 2001. With no more economic growth to ride, the need for cost reductions led to draconian restructuring. Between 2001 and 2003, the number of employees fell from around 95,000 to 35,000. Market capitalization fell from more than $300 billion in 2000 to less than $5 billion two years later. Constrained by a global economy that forced consolidation of both customers and competitors, sales continued to fall and the company was forced to take write-downs of good will from its acquisitions of nearly $16 billion in 2001 alone. Downsizing to the new market realities, R&D investment declined, accelerating the company's free fall.

Having all but abandoned its successful BNR R&D culture to pursue a strategy of buying technology and market share through acquisitions, Nortel had lost its way. It had taken a wrong turn, in the process killing the goose that had laid the golden eggs. In consequence, it had fallen behind, failing to capitalize on the market disruption it created.

In late 2003, the company said it would restate its financial results for 2000, 2001, 2002, and the first half of 2003 to account for almost a billion dollars in liabilities not recorded correctly in earlier audits. The restatements led to an investigation by the U.S. Securities and Exchange Commission, lawsuits, millions of dollars in fines, and the firing of CEO Frank Dunn, along with the CFO and chief controller.

With ongoing downturns in orders and intense competition from North American, European, and low-cost Asian rivals, the downward spiral continued. It couldn't be reversed by the first new CEO, retired U.S. Admiral Bill Owens, nor by his successor, Mike Zafirovinski, who had served as Motorola's president and COO before becoming Nortel's CEO in 2005. With the acquisition strategy in a shambles and without the R&D leadership required for continuous innovation, the window of opportunity to reinvigorate the business closed behind them.

To reduce costs, the company shut down programs, sold some of its business units, abandoned many products under development, especially those that wouldn't generate revenue for years to come, and shrank to a shell of itself. Insecurities reigned and infighting over access to dwindling resources intensified.

Despite the many financial problems, Nortel still managed to generate billions of dollars in sales and retain the number one or two leadership rankings in several market niches, including optical and enterprise data networking. By mid-decade, the company's operating cash flow even turned positive and attempts were made to attract a buyer or a partner to merge with. But given the poor market conditions and the massive liabilities the company carried, all attempts failed. The market crash in the fall of 2008 put an end to all hopes of a turnaround. Nortel Networks filed for bankruptcy protection on January 14, 2009 and requested its stock be delisted from the Toronto Stock Exchange. Once trading at $1,200 per share (before multiple share consolidation to $124), the stock price had fallen to barely more than a dime.

How could Canada's crown jewel, a global powerhouse of technology with more than $30 billion in annual sales, fail so badly after a history of 114 years? What can be learned from the largest bankruptcy in Canadian history? The primary lesson I learned from my adventures applies to *all* organizations powered by innovation: Innovate, adapt, or die.

Rather than lament what was or what might have been, it's more important to celebrate the successes and share the lessons learned during my tenure with a remarkable group of people who accomplished extraordinary things.

Personally, my period of deepest reflection came in May 2001 when Nortel Networks shuttered Design Interpretive, the world-class centre of excellence I had spent my career nurturing as part of our R&D culture for innovation. I can't say I didn't see some downsizing on the horizon, but the way it was done was personally devastating to me and to the people of DI. The organization was expunged and all its 120 employees were tossed onto the street the same day. In so many marketplace battles over the years, the company's vanguard of design-based thinking, armed with user-centric values and whole-product experience, made the critical difference. Now that vanguard was gone. The corporate ship was sinking faster than they could bail water and any definition of a core competency was off the table and low down on any priority list.

Heartbroken, I questioned my career achievements and their relevance. Talking to friends and colleagues, I soon discovered I wasn't alone. Is that all there is? Of course not. While my identity was closely tied to BNR and Nortel, my journey towards personal fulfillment began with the early discovery that the wonderful people who placed their faith in me deserved a return on their investment. My adventure depended on an article of faith in myself that I would, over time, find my place.

I would never have guessed that my adventures would lead to finding my passion for industrial design and morphing from a designer to inventor to champion of R&D and product innovation. Notwithstanding the occasional speed bump, one or two sinkholes, dumb ideas, and constant challenges along the way, I never lost my resolve to stay the course. How else would I have experienced the wonder of a community of high achievers, whose creativity and intelligence produced brilliant innovations in communications?

There was no elixir or magic potion and there were no rules. More often than not, it was just commitment, dedication, and perseverance that carried the day. I worked hard, played hard, and retained my sense of humour as my greatest strategic asset almost to the end. I loved the brain of my natural child and savoured the learning that came from being surrounded by bright people from across Canada and throughout the world who freely shared their knowledge and experience.

From the moment we choose to join an organization we buy into its corporate vision and leadership. We enter into an implied contract of reciprocal trust, loyalty, and shared core values. When it works we love going to work and love what we do. When it doesn't, we feel like we work in a sweatshop. The difference is leadership. The leaders' role is to create the product vision, share their passion, manage the business, and inspire employees to rise to any challenge ahead. Fortunately I worked with enlightened executives who shared their visions, delivered opportunities, and gave me the chance to contribute to corporate success.

With the launch of BNR, we introduced a vision that stood the test of time: "People reaching out to the challenge of bringing the world together through communications…all in the spirit of innovation, dedication, and excellence." It was a global vision that was without borders or boundaries. It inspired adventures that created new wealth and careers for tens of thousands at home and throughout the world. Fueled by the vitality of organizational youth and complemented by enlightened leaders, product innovation was the engine for growth.

Every organization has a gestalt where, by definition, the whole is greater than the sum of its parts. Every product produced is the physical manifestation of the people and organization that produced it. Every product conveys the very soul of the corporation. A vision can embed itself into the corporate culture and impact the spirit of every employee. It must, for without a shared vision how will anyone know where they're headed?

When I joined the corporate culture, I certainly wasn't pursuing the adage of 'follow your dream'. I didn't have one. Along with many of my peers, I was simply following a circuitous route of observation and discovery based on a comparison of things I loved and all the stuff I hated. Being more intuitive than analytical, I tended to find life coaches rather than mentors. Honouring their values and listening to their anecdotes and stories, I discovered my personal sense of place.

I never achieved patience as a virtue and saw red every time I heard "I'm just doing my job" or "I'm doing what I'm told." I could work with (almost) everyone and honoured the golden rule of do unto others as you would have them do unto you. I was in a good company and followed the example set by leaders who honoured and nurtured integrity and trust. I was interested in people, loved to joke around, and enjoyed the company of the guys in the loading dock just as well as the president and all the VPs. We were all members of a community of shared values. Management by fear or yelling at people belonged someplace else.

I loved ideas and was constantly inspired by what could happen when creativity and imagination were applied to problem solving. Ideas are incredibly precious. They are too easily discounted and can have a remarkably short life unless someone has the passion to give them a chance to breathe through exploration. To have real value, an idea needs the passion of an individual or group that can explore concepts and generate prototypes and is empowered to implement the result. From my earliest training as an industrial designer, every sketch was called an "ideation." Never intended as a solution, the ideation opened the mind to expanded possibilities and, thankfully, occasional eureka moments that would lead to product innovation and market success.

Creative problem solving using the tried and true process of problem-solution-benefit stood the test of my time. I look back with a smile when I think that I had so many business cards for doing essentially the same job all through my career.

I was fortunate to find a pathfinder as an employer. Taking initiative was part of my character and I enjoyed being out in front. Sometimes that was just common sense. In other cases, taking initiative meant pursuing an idea knowing that I had the support of exceptional people such as Don Chisholm championing the way. Free to pursue my adventures, my hell-of-a-run career lasted 35 years.

I'm proud of my contributions, especially of adding my industrial design skill and user values to the organization's core competencies. Through creating Design Interpretive, I was able to introduce behavioural research, graphic user interface (GUI), and user-centric design as part of the whole product experience.

I was fortunate to be part of BNR and its Northern parent. Nortel was a great company that reached a richly deserved global status as an innovator and created thousands of new careers in the process. Through vision, passion, and the skills to implement, Nortel became a leading player in a fundamental industry that transformed the very nature of human communications. We fashioned and built a new world of communication with a profound impact on the course of history. We helped redefine forever how we live, learn and work. Recalling a Gershwin song that in this context mixes joy and sadness, I can say, "No, no! They can't take that away from me."

I have come to terms with my success and failures in the quest for relevance and fulfillment. I left my mark. My greatest regret is not achieving a better balance between career and family. Fortunately, I had a great lady at my side and together we managed to nurture out of the nest three terrific kids with enough spunk to accept the world as they find it and to change everything they think needs changing.

It was the career opportunity of a lifetime. I worked with and for amazing men and women who shared common values of trust and integrity and built friendships through thick and thin, often despite strong differences of opinion. Nortel was an exceptional company that ended in sorrow. Many quiet tears, including my own, were shed in private reflection for a future lost. Greatness lost is sad. Having never tried is tragic.

Although each and every one of us left a bit of our heart and soul behind with its demise, our spirit lives on in the legacy embodied where it should be: with the next generation who will build on our history of innovation.

Six months after filing for bankruptcy protection, Nortel Networks declared that it no longer planned to emerge from bankruptcy and would seek buyers for all its business units. Ericsson bought the wireless network business for $1.13 billion and Avaya the enterprise business for almost $700 million. Along with other operating units and buildings up for grabs in one of the biggest asset sales in Canadian history, Nortel raised $3.2 billion.

Then it put its portfolio of patents up for auction. At the time, the company estimated the value of the portfolio at under a billion dollars. Before the auction, Google said it planned to bid $900 million in cash, a stalking-horse figure that set a floor price. But what some called a "rock star consortium" of technology companies that included Apple, Microsoft, RIM, Ericsson, EMC, and Sony outbid Google and purchased about 6,000 patents and patent applications for $4.5 billion. It was the biggest patent auction in history to that date, soon eclipsed by Google buying Motorola's mobility patents for $12.5 billion.

Patents are the currency of the knowledge-based economy, and some observers noted that if Nortel's management had ever realized the value of the treasure trove they were sitting on, bankruptcy might have been avoided. When compared to the billions gained from the fire sale of Nortel's bricks-and-mortar and other assets, the amount is staggering. When all was said and done, the results of BNR's innovative R&D were the most valuable assets the company had and the only assets that will live on. What greater testimony can there be to the value of innovation and ingenuity?

That extraordinary legacy of innovation is a testament to the talents of the thousands of people who contributed to the company's success. Those who spent years within that world-beating corporate culture learned more than a few things about what's important in the business of transforming the world. The lessons learned have value to the new generation of innovators who have the creativity, imagination, and passion to redefine opportunity and the courage to deliver on a vision.

11 LESSONS LEARNED

With so many new innovators emerging in every country and aspiring to leadership, it's incumbent on business's veteran warriors to share whatever wisdom may be found in lessons learned over a long and dedicated campaign. Some may seem obvious, others not so much so. But these lessons apply to any organization—large, small, or start-up—built on the power of innovation. They hold the keys to success in a fast-changing world.

Vision matters. Without it there is no future. As Lewis Carroll said, "If you don't know where you are going, any road will get you there." Without vision, ideas are a commodity like pork bellies and iron ore, everything is an expense, and investment in the future is always the first target of cost reduction.

Due to the vision and foresight of a few, in little more than 30 years, Northern rose from the relative obscurity of a Canadian branch plant to a global industry leader. It went from a wholly owned subsidiary of Bell Canada to a publicly traded company with a market capitalization of more than $300 billion, $30 billion in sales, and 95,000 employees in dozens of countries around the world. It was an icon of innovation and success.

As a regulated monopoly, Bell Canada could have easily drifted along, content with being a safe-buy stock for widows and orphans. The leaders of Bell Canada were not encouraged to be innovators or to take on market discontinuities. But they had vision and demonstrated leadership. They envisioned an opportunity, defined the destination, and set the course.

They may have thought of Ira Gershwin's lyrics, "They all laughed at Christopher Columbus when he said the world was round. They all laughed when Edison recorded sound," but the leaders stepped out in front, braved the laughter, and invested in the future. The implications of their vision cannot be overstated. They created a technology ecosystem that changed human communications. They built from a base of core competencies that were critical to achieving their vision and proceeded on an act of faith. They set a date and believed that, given a nurturing environment and the freedom to create, empowered people would take care of the rest. A clear direction, good faith, and common sense. What a management concept!

Those who discount vision undermine the very spirit of the culture required to produce product innovation. Innovators execute on their visions by applying imagination and creativity to market disruptions and technological discontinuity. They progress as they probe and earn as they learn. Seeing obstacles as opportunity, they simply get on with the task and have fun in the process. In today's world, with never enough money, they move faster than governments and academics can analyze their progress. In spite of barriers-to-entry, innovators will find a way. They always do.

They don't need help in how to succeed. They need help in smashing the barriers and satisfying their insatiable appetite for the best and brightest minds from their national institutions of education. Organizations, indeed nations, that fail to understand that intellectual capital is their greatest strategic asset do so at their own peril and will be condemned to endure the future they created because of their lack of vision and necessary leadership.

Pathfinders matter. Bell's leaders were pathfinders. Imagining the future, they created and nurtured the culture to follow. They attracted new hires and customers by association, leaving competitors to analyze, replicate, and always be one step behind. With the patience and stewardship of a parent, they listened to the sage advice of trusted senior R&D executives backed by a bunch of young upstarts with the passion to tackle the discontinuity of digital technology. They seized the opportunity and created a Digital World, followed by an OPEN World and a Fiber World and decades of innovation.

The values of these pathfinders shaped the very soul of the corporation and impacted every employee. The values embodied the spirit of innovation, dedication, and excellence which became manifest in each product. Empowered and nurtured, everyone loved going to work, celebrated their skill, and did whatever it took to succeed. Arriving as the first industrial designer, feeling the invincibility of youth, I had no idea of what lay in store. Swept up by the contagious vitality and can-do spirit everywhere, I simply jumped in with both feet and quickly discovered the power and pride of an organization built on trust, integrity, and collaboration.

People matter. Innovation and R&D take time and require an environment that nurtures and celebrates the company's core values. Large or small, organizations need to inspire their people and excite them with the opportunity through a reciprocal contract of empowerment, commitment, and passion. It's how an ordinary organization can accomplish extraordinary things. Easier said than done, when such a contract is established, it becomes the reason people love what they do and love going to work. Exhilarated by the challenge and destination, the only real problem is finding a balance between work and personal life. I was fortunate to find the perfect combination of leadership, vision, and people.

Values matter. Bell also transposed their customer-centric and community values to Northern. "Customer first" was their primary metric, and community service the means of commitment and even endearment. Without fanfare, they supported the communities in which they lived, sponsoring charitable events, endowing academic chairs, and incubating the high-tech sector.

Organizations under stress can forget their reason for being. It's the product, first, foremost, and always. R&D, as the lifeblood of corporate success, needs to be part of a corporation's DNA. All products will experience the alpha-to-omega natural maturity cycle. All will have a beginning and an end. Without attention and intervention, the long-term integrity of product innovation efforts will be sacrificed to the short-term expediency of profit margins and manufacturing efficiency, consuming all available R&D resources.

Failure to continuously innovate leads to corporate obsolescence, which is cited in almost every analysis as the primary turning point in any company's downfall. The failure to pursue innovative solutions for customers is a chronic organizational disease, not usually recognized through self-diagnosis and always listed as the primary cause of death in postmortem analysis. Falling one step behind in the innovation race changes an organization's gestalt from a winner to a loser.

Product innovation often means being willing to obsolete or cannibalize your own product. That means taking a leap of faith and having a go-for-it attitude. It means never being satisfied or leaving well enough alone. The organization needs to nurture an environment where innovators can pursue their passion to imagine new opportunities and possibilities, an environment where innovators are empowered to create and the limits to possible product and intellectual property patents seem boundless.

R&D is complex, expensive, multidisciplinary, and a collaborative undertaking that cannot function in fits

and starts. As a corporation's most important investment, the R&D process requires a separate structure of accountability, one free of the profit-and-loss performance metrics of revenues and gross margins. R&D accountability needs to be tracked through budgets, tough schedules, milestones, and regular review. The trusted, nurtured, and empowered employees require the time and space provided by a supportive and secure investment environment. Innovators are competitive and love being first. Given the opportunity, they will meet any challenge.

Tools are toys and the workplace is a playground for innovation. The only thing more satisfying than creating something new is the experience of seeing the labour of love being manufactured and launched into the marketplace. Every market disruption or technological discontinuity creates a massive space for untapped imagination and product innovation, an opening for staying out in front.

Centralized R&D works when the challenge is to create disruptive solutions. If well led and well managed, the tightly integrated and collaborative community allows for the conditions that nurture personal and professional risk taking along with unorthodox thinking. Clearly, a centralized R&D facility needs to be well coupled to the vision and aspiration of the corporation. R&D in a centralized organization must have the leadership and control to champion and execute the corporate product vision. One of Steve Jobs' first interventions on his return to Apple, concerned that the company had lost its way, involved re-centralizing R&D. Regaining control was imperative.

Decentralized R&D can work if the decentralized group is seen as the recipient of new product for manufacture or sustaining development. Natural conflicts between the centralized and distributed groups can be managed through negotiation in R&D allocations.

Distributed R&D does not work when power and the control of the function is vested in manufacturing or regional sales divisions. When power and control of R&D is distributed, especially with local control of R&D investment, the desire for business unit vertical integration will inevitably stifle long-term corporate goals, all in the name of meeting immediate pressures of profit and loss. Over time the distributed management will be subordinated to market pressure for cost reduction and "feature creep," adding features to keep up with competitors while sucking up resources and compressing the planning horizon.

Market leadership cannot be claimed. It has always been a truism to me that real product leadership is an attribute assigned by the testimony of industry customers, competitors, and analysts. It can never be taken for granted. Real leadership is attained through the passion to reach, to accept and manage risk, and to create and follow a vision. Leadership becomes the natural outcome of both adhering to these principles and delivering on the promises embedded in the vision. Lost product momentum can lead the market to ask questions such as, "Are they a one trick pony?" or "Have they run out of ideas?" The sentiment can create a wait-and-see position by customers, while opening an opportunity for competitors.

Success is a measure of a corporation's past hard work and innovative achievements. Success is a trailing indicator, but is enjoyed and consumed in the present. That can breed arrogance and, more insidiously, complacency and sloth in the top echelons of a corporation. Every successful company is susceptible to becoming fat and lazy without a healthy dose of paranoia for market disruptions. Unfortunately, executives and board members can become increasingly remote from the culture that created the product innovation that generated their success. They stop listening to internal voices and become mesmerized by the adulation of business media, a group remote from the sources of a company success. Board members and executives can succumb to the sin of greed and fall prey to the deadliest sin of all: reveling in one's own hubris.

Fun matters. Fun that often included mischief was part of our behavior at BNR. To me, loving my job was synonymous with fun. A lot of laughter is the best medicine for the mental health of an organization and is also a means of releasing creativity, imagination, and innovation. Laughter excites the senses when they are dulled by the natural tensions created by stress and the frustrations that come with the challenges of solving even the most interesting problems. Laughter is a barometer of organizational spirit. I learned that if I wasn't having fun I should stop, ask why, and address the reason. More often than not, it was because the solution was inadequate, or was the wrong thing to do, or I was simply afraid to admit failure.

On one occasion, sensing a lack of enthusiasm for a languishing project, I asked the group to close their eyes, lower their heads, and raise their hands if they were having fun. None was raised. Discussion provided a rarely revealed truth: admission of failure creates job insecurity and generates fear of public exposure or of signaling incompetence. We publicly cancelled the project, declared it a success, liberated the remaining budget and staff to a new exploratory project of their choice, and announced an after-work celebration of pizza and beer. Fun and laughter returned, along with creativity. Fun is a soft metric that is difficult to quantify, but can stimulate ordinary people to accomplish extraordinary things through collaboration.

Recognition and celebrations matter. Starting with a simple "thank you," the action of celebrating or marking an occasion or accomplishment is another soft metric, one that is the easiest to do and most often overlooked. From my experience, lots of small celebrations are better than the big traditional ones. We once declared an un-celebration when we had nothing to celebrate, much like the un-birthday at the Mad Hatter's tea party. It just felt good. A simple act of bringing together a dedicated community builds the nurtured fraternity already in place and, most importantly, creates a return on investment for the people and project that is immediate and cumulative.

Expenditures for small celebrations are often the first thing to be cut at the first sign of financial pressure. Good faith and common sense might suggest that cutting the means to keep people focused and happy while dealing with the challenges of the tasks at hand would be the very last thing to do. But in such circumstances, silliness and perverse logic usually prevail. These perversions in logic have kept my love for Lewis Carroll's literary nonsense alive and well. How can one not savour the scene from *Alice's Adventures in Wonderland* where the Queen of Hearts pronounces at the trial of the Knave of Hearts, "Sentence first—verdict afterwards"?

Innovation creates new wealth because it creates new value. By stepping up to the challenge of innovating, new opportunities and new careers are created. While nurturing a culture of innovation will challenge national education programs to produce people that can compete on a global playing field, such a culture will also attract new international capital investment. The resulting new product cascade will create opportunities for individual fulfillment and relevance, and attract highly talented people to the enriched community.

A culture of innovation creates a domino effect where small businesses can expand. Small businesses are the single largest source of new private sector jobs, but we cannot and should not take them for granted. While loyal to their community and nation, young people are inevitably in the search for relevance and fulfillment. Yet, as it has always been and always will be, young people are impatient and nomadic by nature. If they cannot find or produce an ecosystem which nurtures innovation at home they will, in frustration, follow the money and migrate, leaving an impoverished community behind.

The never-ending conflict of expense versus investment is the greatest challenge to any organization whose success depends on innovation and R&D. Whether large or small, that natural conflict is where the fight for power and control can rear its ugly head, particularly when the business sees signs of trouble ahead and short-term expediency prevails.

Anyone who has ever worked in private enterprise knows how fast the culture can shift over positive to negative cash flow. In a world where cash is king, fretters emerge from the woodwork and start counting heads and paper clips. While they focus on operating expenses and return on sales, they forget about the return on intellectual capital, the investment that creates product success in the first place. Without the right leadership, they will defer the future and risk falling behind, which they usually do. The battle of managing R&D as an expense versus an investment cost two Nortel CEOs their jobs.

Corporate culture, easy to see but hard to measure, takes time to create but very little time to destroy. BNR's employees bought into the company's vision as an act of faith and continued their commitment to the original contract through thick and thin. The commitment of the employees was not based on job security but on their love for what they did and where they did it.

I met few, if any, innovators who defined success in terms of personal financial wealth. Fulfillment came from having the opportunity to do what they loved and being surrounded by kindred spirits who shared their passion. Fairly compensated, they defined return on investment as personal fulfillment and relevance to executing and delivering on the corporate promise.

Personal fulfillment meant passion and commitment, pride in accomplishments, providing for their families, and contributing to the community. These dedicated people created extraordinary things. They merit celebration.

Here endeth the lessons.

12 THE POWER OF PURPLE

George Smyth, Irving Ebert, and I all retired all around the same time. The decision for me was relatively easy since I had clearly become an outsider without power or influence. While I can't speak for the others, I suspect they could read the same writing on the wall.

About a year later, Irving and his wife hosted an elegant, candle-lit gourmet dinner party for George and me and our spouses featuring excellent wines from his extensive cellar collection. After the meal, the three of us retired (pun intended) to his home library for gentlemen's coffee, cognac, and cigars, the ladies having zero interest in what would inevitably be shoptalk. Irving suggested that, based on our cumulative experience, we needed to do something for fun. By the end of the discussion, and with the benefit of more cognac, we created an investment group, Purple Angel, with our headquarters at Ralph's Diner and Gas Bar. Close to BNR's central labs, Ralph's had for decades been the closest place for late-night food or early-morning breakfasts.

We invited four former colleagues (who all had purple blood) to join us, and over the next few years we invested in local Ottawa-area start-ups. Breaking ranks with conventional angel groups, we did not create an investment pool. Based on our evaluation of the business, each angel decided his personal level of dollar contribution. In the spirit of all for one and one for all, we all committed to mentor the start-up, no matter the investment. Only those members who contributed cash received an equity position. We only had two other rules: one, we wouldn't invest unless we could also bring an interested venture capitalist to the table; and, two, the project had to be fun.

We wanted to continue a long-standing BNR tradition of contributing to the Ottawa community. Ottawa had always been the heart and brain of Nortel's R&D powerhouse and BNR had always been a prime advocate of collaboration with the R&D resources active within all the communities in which the company operated. Bonnie Jackson, the first Northern pinstripe I ever met, became BNR's first director of university liaison and, as a result of his initiatives, BNR went on to invest in university research and to endow academic research chairs. It was a win-win situation that also bolstered our ability to recruit the best and brightest engineers and software analysts. Millions were invested. BNR was incubating as it supported the high-tech community growing around our campus during the last third of the 20th century.

While BNR was gone in the early 2000s, there were thousands of former employees out on the street anxious to try their hand at becoming entrepreneurs. The displaced employees with nothing to lose had access to lots of money, given the investment environment at that time. Available dollars peaked in Ottawa during 2000, estimated at $1.38 billion. The region was still reputed to be Silicon Valley North.

During the next few years, I certainly had fun with my friends. That was not always the case with the start-ups. Lousy listeners, they just seemed to want our money. George and I left about the same time for similar, if not the same, reasons. We agreed it was no longer fun and, in spite of claims, the start-ups didn't really want our help after they had tapped our wallets. The other common reason was that with the collapse of Nortel's shares, we needed to substantially lower our investment risk. In contrast, Irving, who George and I affectionately named "Arch Angel," loved the work and kept the group going.

Over the decade, the venture capital pool in Ottawa declined, dropping by about 50 percent by 2002 alone. By 2005, it was down to approximately $300 million and down to an estimated $150-$200 million by 2013. By 2010, the hype and rhetoric around Ottawa as the high-tech capital was simply hype. The action had moved to Waterloo, though Ottawa could still drive innovation. But the hangover from the demise of Nortel and the thousands unceremoniously dumped into the labour pool had at least stabilized.

During the investment drought, the dynamics changed from the eager start-ups raking in the dough to a prolonged period when the new entrepreneurs would do anything to keep their ventures afloat, indulging in the never-ending cycle of chasing money, downsizing, pursuing second and third rounds of financing, consolidating, and suffering an ever declining equity position for the founders. As the investment dried up, some venture capitalists left town. Many angels took their losses and retired for a second time. In spite of the drought, Purple Angel remained alive and managed a reasonably successful hit rate in line with industry averages.

It was during this time that I began to notice a 10-year technology generation gap. A generation may be considered about 25 years, but in technology that's a lifetime. The people who had just wanted Purple Angel's money were an older cohort. But the younger generation, who I think of as "the kids," born in the 1980s and coming into their own in the new millennium, have a different outlook and a different attitude. These are young people whose spirit and values are contagious. They give me hope—even the certainty—that innovation is alive and well. We are in good hands.

The media hype of pundits centers on the implications of digital media, social networking, and who will build the next killer app in the smart phone wars. But they are merely analyzing the present and the past, scratching the surface of the knowledge economy. They are forecasting a future while looking through a rear-view mirror, when backcasting, as practiced by the Corporate Design Group, can reveal far greater truths.

The up-starts already know that they need to generate cash flow from early adopting customers while achieving positive cash flow from operations. They understand that innovation requires implementation and execution with discipline. Frustrated by the onerous process of government programs and venture capital investment that too often leaves founders and employees as diluted minority shareholders, they have created new sources of equity funding.

As the breadth and depth of information expands and the speed of access increases, collaboration transcends borders and kindred spirits in applied science are forming their own communities, developing an innovation ecosystem independent of time and space. Consensus is compressed and innovation is liberated for those with the knowledge and skills to execute. Untethered, they are only constrained by the access and interval to funding. In their unrelenting adventure for relevance and fulfillment, they will prevail.

The corporate world has changed and because of global recessions and fragile national economies, innovators no longer look for a life-long career with one company. Maybe that's a good thing... and as it should be. With the prospect of multiple employers, innovators know the quest for relevance and fulfillment means investing in themselves, confirming what they love to do, and finding a collaborative community that shares their values. The wide-open space has no limits to the creativity and imagination of those with the passion to define where the opportunity lies and to go for it.

Innovation is the raison *raison d'être* in the R&D cultures of applied science, for example, including physics, chemistry, biology, medicine, and engineering. Given financial shortages, they are becoming increasingly untethered from the conventional umbilical cord of academic and government funds. Will crowd funding be part of these innovators' future? Loving what they do, collaborative, and never content with the status quo, they are taking innovation to a new level by cross-fertilization and interdisciplinary application.

Consider the implications of their simply adding the prefix bio: biophysics, biochemistry, and bioengineering. We stand to see new products that will again challenge our understanding of how to work and live. While hospital physicians are using iPads to consolidate everything from patient records to lab tests to state-of-the-art diagnostics, their colleagues at Harvard are experimenting with the viability of storing large amounts of data on DNA molecules as a digital storage medium. Others are growing arteries and veins for transplant using a patient's stem cells and DNA. Can custom pharmaceuticals and smart transplants be far behind?

As the several applied science fields converge and achieve a meta- or hyper-state, the higher order will create the next market disruption and technology discontinuity, opening the way for even more innovation beyond anything we can imagine today.

The challenge to business innovators and governments alike is to adopt or adapt the spirit defined so many years ago at BNR: People, reaching out to the challenge of bringing the world together, all in the spirit of innovation, dedication, and excellence. Embracing the power of purple can help define new paths forward and provide sustenance and support along the way.

The choices are clear for all players: compete or fall one step behind. The adage applies equally to industry leaders, start-ups, and national governments: innovate and adapt or die. I remain an optimist. Regardless of barriers to entry, the new generation of innovators will find a way as they always do. Driven by passion and the commitment to do whatever it takes, they will find the needed investment and create new wealth through market disruptions and technology discontinuities, once again changing how we live and work.

I can hear the voices of colleagues, joined by the new generation, rising in chorus longing to ignite the flame of innovation that never dies. I hear them saying, as I noted long ago: Without reach, there is no challenge. Without risk, there is no reward. Without vision, there is no future.

INDEX

Fitzgerald, Edmund B. (78, 81-83, 85, 105, 108, 113, 137, 146)
Frischkorn, Norbert (79, 80)
Fuller, Buckminster (73)
Gates, Bill (167)
Graham Bell, Alexander (27, 33)
Gray, Elisha (27)
Gustaf, King Carl (141, 187)
Herman Miller (73)
Hewat, Brian (139, 142-144, 147, 155, 160, 163, 165)
Hopper, Joyce (73)
House, David (179, 180)
Hudson, Des (83, 87, 88, 91, 92, 94, 98, 99, 115, 117, 143)
Iacocca, Lee (154)
J. Walter Thompson (95, 96)
Jackson, Bonnie (20)
Jackson, Bonnie (210)
Jobs, Steve (203)
Kennedy, Jim (32)
Kipling, Rudyard (16)
Kyles, Jim (57, 58)
Langton, Ray (114, 116, 149)
Lastman, Mel "Badboy" (20)
Leblanc, Velma (149)
Lewis, Carroll (199, 206)
Light, Walter F. (62, 75, 77-79, 80, 82, 85, 136, 146, 157, 171, 180)
Lightfoot, Gordon (78)
Lindsay, Don (178)
Lobb, John (28, 56, 57, 59, 62, 63, 67, 72)
Long, James (109, 143, 173, 180)
Lotochinski, Eugene (76, 77, 88)
Lucas, Helmut(26, 27)
Lucente, Edward (109, 114, 121, 135, 136)
Luff, Peter (38)
Mahan, John (44)
Marquez, Vernon (32)

Marsalis, Wynton (120)
Matthews, Terry (38, 83, 151)
McCann/Erickson (34)
McCaw, Craig (170)
McDonald, Art (173)
McLuhan, Marshall (69)
McNealy, Scott (167)
Mead, Syd (73,-75)
Merrills, Roy (107, 143)
Monty, Jean (135-139, 143-146, 148, 150, 152, 157, 158, 160, 169)
Moss, Bill (28)
Muller-Thyme, Bernard (69)
Munsell, Albert (17)
Nelson, George (73, 74)
Nevitt, Barrington (69)
Newman, Peter C. (145, 147, 153)
Noyes, Elliot (73)
Owens, Bill (191)
Payette, Julie (175)
Peterson, Don (143)
Pfeffer, Robert (105, 116)
Rams, Dieter (109)
Roth, John (90, 131, 132, 140, 143, 144, 148, 154, 160-162, 165, 167, 169, 170, 173, 174, 176, 177, 179, 180, 184, 186, 187)
Sadler, Graham (38)
Sakus, Dana (183, 184)
Sakus, Gedas (165, 167, 173, 182, 183, 184)
Schmidt, Arno (114)
Scrivener, Robert C. (24, 33, 39, 51, 56, 62, 63, 65, 66, 68, 136, 171)
Shah of Iran (141)
Shiu, Charlie (122)
Smyth, George (105, 112, 116-118, 125, 126, 128, 140, 142, 144, 155, 160, 163, 165, 209, 210)
Sottsass, Ettore (71, 73)

ABOUT THE AUTHOR

John Tyson is an industrial designer, inventor, angel investor and accomplished senior executive who spent over 35 years with Bell-Northern Research (BNR) and Nortel Networks. During this time he focused on product design, R&D, marketing, and advanced technology. His principles on user-centered design, innovation, and design-based thinking have been detailed in numerous publications and his work has been featured in museums and galleries including the Museum of Modern Art in New York, the National Art Gallery of Canada, the Canadian Museum of Science and Technology, the Canadian Museum of Civilization, and the Toronto Design Exchange (DX). His work has also been featured on two Canadian postage stamps.

www.ingramcontent.com/pod-product-compliance
Lightning Source LLC
Chambersburg PA
CBHW060547200326
41521CB00007B/522

*9 780993 619304 *